Cambridge Certificate of Proficiency in English 3

WITH ANSWERS

Examination papers from University of Cambridge ESOL Examinations: English for Speakers of Other Languages

CAMBRIDGE
UNIVERSITY PRESS

PUBLISHED BY THE PRESS SYNDICATE OF THE UNIVERSITY OF CAMBRIDGE
The Pitt Building, Trumpington Street, Cambridge, United Kingdom

CAMBRIDGE UNIVERSITY PRESS
The Edinburgh Building, Cambridge, CB2 2RU, UK
40 West 20th Street, New York, NY 10011–4211, USA
477 Williamstown Road, Port Melbourne, VIC 3207, Australia
Ruiz de Alarcón 13, 28014 Madrid, Spain
Dock House, The Waterfront, Cape Town 8001, South Africa

http://www.cambridge.org

First published 2004

Printed in the United Kingdom at the University Press, Cambridge

ISBN 0 521 543851 Student's Book
ISBN 0 521 54386X Student's Book with answers
ISBN 0 521 543916 Self-study Pack
ISBN 0 521 543878 Teacher's Book
ISBN 0 521 543886 Set of 2 Cassettes
ISBN 0 521 543894 Set of 2 Audio CDs

Contents

Thanks and acknowledgements

The publishers are grateful to the following for permission to reproduce copyright material. It has not always been possible to identify the sources of all the material used and in such cases the publishers would welcome information from the copyright owners.

For the extract on p. 5: from *The Travelling Hornplayer* by Barbara Trapido (Penguin Books Ltd, 1999) Copyright © Barbara Trapido, 1999; for the article 'Language' on p. 5: © RSA *Journal*, Vol CXLV No 5477 (p. 38), March 1997; for the extract on p. 6: 'Vervet monkeys' from *The Trouble with Science* by Robin Dunbar, published by Faber and Faber Ltd; for the extract on p. 12: from *The Orchard on Fire* by Shene Mackay, published by Heinemann. Used by permission of The Random House Group Limited; for the article on p. 16: 'The ways we have changed', by permission of the Readers Digest Association, *Marvels and Mysteries of the Human Mind*, © 1997; for p. 30: adapted from *The boy in the bubble – a biography of Paul Simon* by Patrick Humphries, published by Pan Macmillan Ltd, 1988; for p. 32: 'Self-help books' by Giles Whittell published in *The Times*, 22/12/1997, and p. 87: 'Film-makers' by Geoff Brown in *The Times*, 13/02/1997, © NI Syndication London; for p. 33 adapted from 'The Trouble with Autobiographies', written by J M Coetzee, Arts & Books Supplements, *The Daily Telegraph*, 6/11/1999; for p. 34: 'Dashiell Hammett's detective stories' from *The Life of Dashiell Hammett*, by Diane Johnson; for the article on p. 35: adapted from 'If you want to win', by Steve Jones, *The Daily Telegraph*, 4/12/1996 and for p. 90: adapted from 'Ernest Shackleton as a model of good management' by Eluned Price, *The Daily Telegraph*, 12/09/1998 @Telegraph Group Limited; for p. 36: extract from *Advertising on Trial* (1993) by Jim Ring published by Pearson Education Limited; *The Economist* for p. 43:

from 'Cloudbursting' © The Economist Newspaper Limited, London 21/08/1999; for the extract on p. 48: from *The Classic Fairy Tale* by Opie, Iona and Peter (1974), reprinted by permission of Oxford University Press; for the article on p. 58: extracted from *Cooking for Friends* © 1991 Raymond Blanc. Reproduced by permission of Headline Book Publishing Limited; for p. 61: 'Miss Fogerty', from *More Stories from Thrush Green* by Miss Read (Penguin Books, 1985) Copyright © Miss Read; for the article on p. 64: from *Aesthetics? The Big Questions* edited by Carolyn Korsmeyer (1998) Blackwell Publishing Ltd; for p. 84: 'Every Picture tells a story'. An extract from an essay first published in *Prospect Magazine* November 1996; www.prospect-magazine.co.uk; for p. 85: extract by B Bettleheim from 'Recollections and Reflections' (1990) published by Thames & Hudson; for the extract on p. 86: 'Film Studios' from *Frequent Hearses* written by Edmund Crispin, reproduced with the kind permission of Rights Limited. Copyright © 1950 Rights Limited, a Chorion company. All rights reserved; for the extract on p. 88: from 'A Trinity' by William Trevor from *The Collected Stories* published by Penguin.

Art Directors & Trip: p. C5 (2B), C7 (3E) and C8 (4C); Bubbles Photo Library: p. C9 (4D); Corbis: pp. C4 (2A and 2B), C5 (2A and 2C), C6 (3A) and C9 (4E and 4F); Getty Images: p. C6 (3B and 3C); Rex Features: pp. C3, C4 (2C) and C7 (3D and 3F); John Walmsley Photo Library: p. C8 (4A and 4B).

Picture research by Jacqui Rivers

Cover design by Dunne & Scully

The cassettes and audio CDs which accompany this book were recorded at Studio AVP, London

To *the student*

This book is for candidates preparing for the University of Cambridge ESOL Examinations Certificate of Proficiency in English (CPE). The CPE examination is recognised by the majority of British universities for English language entrance requirements.

This collection of four complete practice tests comprises past papers from the Cambridge Certificate of Proficiency in English examination and reflects the most recent CPE specifications (introduced in December 2002). You can practise these tests on your own or with the help of your teacher.

The CPE examination is part of a group of examinations developed by Cambridge ESOL called the Cambridge Main Suite. The Main Suite consists of five examinations which have similar characteristics but which are designed for different levels of English ability. Within the five levels, CPE is at Level C2 in the Council of Europe's *Common European Framework of Reference for Languages: Learning, teaching, assessment* and Level 3 in the UK National Qualifications Framework.

Examination	Common European Framework	UK National Qualifications Framework
CPE Certificate of Proficiency in English	C2	**3**
CAE Certificate in Advanced English	C1	2
FCE First Certificate in English	B2	1
PET Preliminary English Test	B1	Entry 3
KET Key English Test	A2	Entry 2

The CPE examination consists of five papers:

Paper 1	Reading	1 hour 30 minutes
Paper 2	Writing	2 hours
Paper 3	Use of English	1 hour 30 minutes
Paper 4	Listening	40 minutes (approximately)
Paper 5	Speaking	19 minutes

Paper 1   Reading

This paper consists of four parts with 40 questions, which take the form of three multiple-choice tasks and a gapped text task. Part 1 contains three short texts, Part 2 contains four short texts and Parts 3 and 4 each contain one longer text. The texts are taken from fiction, non-fiction, journals, magazines, newspapers, and promotional and informational materials. This paper is designed to test candidates' ability to understand the meaning of written English at word, phrase, sentence, paragraph and whole text level.

Paper 2   Writing

This paper consists of two writing tasks in a range of formats (e.g. letter, report, review, article, essay, proposal). Candidates are asked to complete two tasks, writing between 300 and 350 words for each. Part 1 (Question 1) consists of one compulsory task based on instructions and a short text. Part 2 (Questions 2–5) consists of one task which candidates select from a choice of four. Question 5 has a task on one of each of three set texts. Assessment is based on achievement of task, range and accuracy of vocabulary and grammatical structures, organisation and appropriacy of register and format.

Paper 3   Use of English

This paper consists of five parts with 44 questions. These take the form of an open cloze, a word formation task, gapped sentences, key word transformations and two texts with comprehension questions and a summary writing task. The paper is designed to assess candidates' ability to demonstrate knowledge and control of the language system by completing these tasks which are at text and sentence level.

Paper 4   Listening

This paper consists of four parts with 28 questions, which take the form of two multiple-choice tasks, a sentence-completion task and a three-way matching task. Part 1 contains four short extracts and Parts 2 to 4 each contain one longer text. The texts are audio-recordings based on a variety of sources including interviews, discussions, lectures, conversations and documentary features. The paper is designed to assess candidates' ability to understand the meaning of spoken English, to extract information from a spoken text and to understand speakers' attitudes and opinions.

Paper 5   Speaking

The Speaking Test consists of three parts, which take the form of an interview section, a collaborative task and individual long turns with follow-up discussion. The test is designed to elicit a wide range of language from both candidates. Candidates are examined in pairs by two examiners, an Interlocutor and an Assessor. The Assessor awards a mark based on the following criteria: Grammatical Resource, Lexical Resource, Discourse Management, Pronunciation and Interactive Communication. The Interlocutor provides a global mark for the whole test.

Marks and results

The five CPE papers total 200 marks, after weighting. Each paper is weighted to 40 marks.

Your overall CPE grade is based on the total score gained in all five papers. It is not necessary to achieve a satisfactory level in all five papers in order to pass the examination. Certificates are given to candidates who pass the examination with grade A, B or C. A is the highest. The minimum successful performance in order to achieve a grade C corresponds to about 60% of the total marks. D and E are failing grades. Your Statement of Results will include a graphical display of your performance in each paper. These are shown against the scale Exceptional – Good – Borderline – Weak and indicate your relative performance in each paper.

Further information

For more information about CPE or any other Cambridge ESOL examination contact:

University of Cambridge
ESOL Examinations
1 Hills Road
Cambridge
CB1 2EU
United Kingdom

Tel: +44 1223 553355
Fax: +44 1223 460278
Email: ESOLHelpdesk@UCLES.org.uk
Website: www.CambridgeESOL.org

In some areas, this information can also be obtained from the British Council.

Test 1

PAPER 1   READING (1 hour 30 minutes)

Part 1

For questions **1–18**, read the three texts below and decide which answer (**A**, **B**, **C** or **D**) best fits each gap.

Mark your answers **on the separate answer sheet**.

Einstein

Stop anyone in the street and ask them to name a scientist, and the chances are they'll think of Albert Einstein. His face is used to advertise products with intellectual **(1)** .... , from computers to encyclopaedias.

Most people know little of what Einstein did, except that he developed some mysterious theories under the heading 'relativity', which are famous for being incomprehensible, and for coming up with bizarre predictions that **(2)** .... counter to everyday experience.

Einstein was part of a gigantic **(3)** .... forward in scientific thinking, an intellectual revolution that **(4)** .... the birth of twentieth century science. Physicists and mathematicians were trying to create a new, more rational description of the universe by studying relationships between matter and the forces of nature.

Einstein **(5)** .... his profound and far-reaching contributions simply by looking again at the nature of the fundamentals: time, space, matter and energy. Previous descriptions had depended on Isaac Newton's view of a universe in which stars and planets moved in an absolute framework of space and time. Einstein **(6)** .... this notion, saying that time and space were not absolute but relative.

1 **A** suppositions   **B** connotations   **C** assumptions   **D** inferences

2 **A** drive   **B** fall   **C** flow   **D** run

3 **A** flight   **B** leap   **C** dive   **D** vault

4 **A** ushered   **B** notified   **C** heralded   **D** declared

5 **A** gave   **B** laid   **C** offered   **D** made

6 **A** overthrew   **B** overtook   **C** overwhelmed   **D** overran

Young Readers

Throughout our childhoods, Lydia and I distrusted any prize-winning book because we knew it would be worthy; and for 'worthy', **(7)** …. 'boring', we thought.

While our mother had been inclined to abhor our philistinism in tones of despising innuendo, our father would cheerfully dish us out tenpences, chapter by chapter, as inducements to make us **(8)** …. our eyes over the occasional improving volume. Or he would **(9)** …. the odd superior book in amongst our Christmas and birthday presents, labelled in bold marker pen, 'This Book is NOT Literature'. Though we **(10)** …. most of his offerings as 'boys' books', he did, in this way, **(11)** …. us to some shorter works of decent fiction and, just once, to a well-known **(12)** …. of verse.

7 A interpret	**B** read	**C** consider	**D** define
8 A chuck	**B** throw	**C** hurl	**D** cast
9 A link	**B** weave	**C** slip	**D** fold
10 A dismissed	**B** disqualified	**C** discredited	**D** disclaimed
11 A reveal	**B** expose	**C** unveil	**D** disclose
12 A album	**B** periodical	**C** manual	**D** anthology

Language

'The origin of human language is truly secret and marvellous,' wrote Jacob Grimm in 1851. The marvellous secret has long proved a launch pad for strange ideas. 'Primitive man was likely to make sounds like "meuh" when **(13)** …. danger,' claimed Charles Caller in 1928. '"Meuh" has a plaintive sound. The human who wandered over a hostile land inhabited by awesome beasts **(14)** …. desperate noises, and languages have preserved some echo of his lamentation such as *malaria* meaning "fever" or the Latin *mors* meaning "death".'

Faced with such weird speculations, many avoided the topic, regarding it as a playground for cranks, but recently, language origin and evolution have become key research areas. Language probably developed in East Africa, around 100,000 years ago. **(15)** …. , speech was used for friendly interaction, and was an important tool in power **(16)** …. . Information-swapping was probably not an important original **(17)** …. – contrary to the views of philosopher John Locke, who spoke of language as a 'great conduit' for **(18)** …. knowledge.

13 A feeling	**B** sensing	**C** suffering	**D** fighting
14 A screeched	**B** cried	**C** called	**D** uttered
15 A In conclusion	**B** As a consequence	**C** In the main	**D** Despite this
16 A struggles	**B** wars	**C** strikes	**D** contests
17 A argument	**B** service	**C** role	**D** thought
18 A dispatching	**B** conveying	**C** teaching	**D** passing

You are going to read four extracts which are all concerned in some way with animals. For questions **19–26**, choose the answer (**A**, **B**, **C** or **D**) which you think fits best according to the text.

Mark your answers **on the separate answer sheet**.

Vervet monkeys

Cheney and Seyfarth describe how one day the dominant male in the group of vervet monkeys they were studying noticed a strange male hanging around in a neighbouring grove of trees. The stranger's intentions were quite obvious: he was sizing up the group in order to join it. If he succeeded, it was more than likely that the incumbent male would be ousted from his position of privilege. With the vervet equivalent of a stroke of genius, the male hit on the ideal ploy to keep the stranger away from his group. As soon as the strange male descended from the grove of trees to try to cross the open ground that separated his grove from the one in which the group was feeding, he gave an alarm call that vervets use to signal the sighting of a leopard nearby. The stranger shot back into the safety of his trees. As the day wore on, this was repeated every time the stranger made a move in the group's direction. All was going swimmingly until the male made a   line 12 crucial mistake: after successfully using the ploy several times, he gave the leopard alarm call while himself nonchalantly walking across open ground.

19   The writer describes the dominant male's tactic as

    A inspirational.
    B ambitious.
    C hazardous.
    D impudent.

20   What aspect of the situation is emphasised by the use of the word 'swimmingly' (line 12)?

    A the tension
    B the danger
    C the humour
    D the charm

What Cats Catch

In a recent survey, people in the 173-household English village of Felmersham collected their cats' prey. Over one year their seventy cats produced over 1,000 prey items. A professor in America saw these figures and worked out that on this basis the cat population of Britain must be killing 100 million birds and small mammals each year!

The mesmeric effect of big numbers seems to have stultified reason. It is not realistic just to multiply the number of catches of these rural cats by the entire cat population of Britain. Most cats are town cats with small ranges, and catch fewer items of prey than the cats in this survey. The key question should have been this: are the numbers sustainable? The answer would seem to be yes.

In winter many householders feed birds, while garden trees and buildings provide nesting sites, and in this way the bird population is kept at well above 'natural' levels. The survey found that the cat is a significant predator, but not that it is devastating Britain's bird population.

21   What is suggested about the American professor?

   A   He did not use his common sense.
   B   He did not understand English village life.
   C   He misunderstood the results of the survey.
   D   He asked the wrong questions.

22   What point is made about cats in Britain?

   A   They are no more dangerous than other predators.
   B   They have an effect on the numbers of birds.
   C   They are not increasing in numbers.
   D   They do less harm in rural areas.

A Buffalo's Day

The buffaloes are, as it were, the marshman's lifeline, and they are cherished accordingly. At each dawn the buffaloes, who have been sleeping on the buffalo platform or quite frequently round the fire with their owners, leave, infinitely slowly and wearily, their wallowing progress continually punctuated with despairing groans, for the distant reed beds beyond the open water. For a long time they stand on the edge of the platform, groaning to each other of the infinite fatigue of the coming day, until at last the leader takes a ponderous pace forward and subsides into the water.

Once in the water a deep lassitude once more descends upon the party, as if they had by now forgotten their intention and they may wallow there with low notes of complaint for many minutes. The movements that at length remove them from the immediate vicinity of the house are so gradual as to pass practically unnoticed, but finally they are swimming, so low in the water that their noses seem held above it by a last effort of ebbing strength, their rolling eyes proclaiming that this is the end at last and that they are drowning. So, patient and protesting and more or less submerged, they spend the day among the reeds and the bulrushes, grazing leisurely upon such green shoots as their antediluvian heads may find at eye level.

23 The writer states that the marshmen

    A worship the buffaloes.
    B look after the buffaloes carefully.
    C treat the buffaloes better than they do people.
    D guard the buffaloes closely.

24 What sort of sounds do the buffaloes make?

    A melancholy
    B drowsy
    C lazy
    D irate

PICASSO, Pablo *The soles* 1940 Oil on canvas
Scottish National Gallery of Modern Art

Picasso tended to paint those things that surrounded him, and in the early spring of 1940, he painted several fish still lifes while he was staying in the fishing port of Royan. The ostensible subject of the painting is a fishmonger's slab with a crab, and a pair of scales containing two or three soles. In spite of their predicament these sea creatures look very much still alive. It is not very easy to read the painting because Picasso has treated the composition in terms of a flat pattern of overlapping and interlocking transparent planes. This, the thin delicately brushed paint, and the cool, undemonstrative colours give the painting the appearance of an underwater world of slow-moving calm and harmony. But this is disturbed by what seems to be an impending battle between the fish, baring their teeth, and the crab, with its open claws. Those sharp, pointed forms are echoed by the scales. Even the chain going round one of the fish takes on a more sinister aspect. There is an undercurrent of menace and barely suppressed violence that gives the picture a symbolic edge.

25   The writer suggests that the idea behind this painting

    A   was not typical of Picasso's work.
    B   is not immediately obvious.
    C   is revealed by Picasso's painting technique.
    D   was influenced by contemporary taste.

26   The writer says the creatures in the painting look as if

    A   they have just been caught.
    B   they have been trying to escape.
    C   they are still swimming in the sea.
    D   they are about to fight each other.

Part 3

You are going to read an extract from the autobiography of the lyricist Tim Rice. Seven paragraphs have been removed from the extract. Choose from the paragraphs **A–H** the one which fits each gap (**27–33**). There is one extra paragraph which you do not need to use.

Mark your answers **on the separate answer sheet**.

TIM RICE

I was ushered into the young man's drawing room, an oasis of cultured sanity surrounded by what appeared to be a quite shambolic cluster of rooms in which the less enterprising members of the family operated. Moving from the kitchen to his parlour was an upgrade from economy to business class.

27	

His name was Andrew Lloyd Webber. He had won a scholarship to Magdalen College, Oxford, to read history, and he had nine months to kill before going up, during which time he intended to become England's answer to the composer Richard Rodgers.

28	

Consequently, when Andrew suggested a completely new insane ambition for me, i.e. to become as famous a lyricist as Oscar Hammerstein, I had no qualms about giving it a go. This was partly because within ten minutes of our introduction, he was at the piano and had played me three tunes he had composed – I could tell that he was good. Very good.

29	

I had little to impress him with in return, other than instant praise for his music and a bona fide, actually released, seven-inch single of a song I had written (both words and music) with which an unknown pop group had dealt the final blow to their moribund career by recording three months previously. We parted, promising to meet again and to write something together. I was still more interested in the charts than in the West End theatre, but told myself on the bus back to my flat that I had just met somebody of rare ability and determination, and I would be mad to miss

out on being a sidekick to a chap who was clearly going to take the musical theatre by storm, probably by next week.

30	

The next day, back at my desk in the office where I was training to become a solicitor, the brief certainty I had enjoyed of a life in show business with Andrew Lloyd Webber had faded somewhat. I would of course continue to keep an eye on the small ads in *Melody Maker* for groups needing a vocalist, and would turn out a few more three-chord songs tailored not to expose the limitations of my voice, but it was still odds-on that eventually I would stagger through my exams and wind up a respectable lawyer by the time I was twenty-five.

31	

But in the meantime I felt I had nothing to lose by seeing Andrew again. It would be fun to go and see a musical with him, to write words that aped musical lyricists rather than pop stars. And Andrew was a fascinating individual who talked of *Good Food Guides* and Victorian architecture, besides supporting Leyton Orient football team.

32	

The idea was the life of Dr Thomas Barnardo, the nineteenth century philanthropist who founded the orphanages that bear his name. His story was a worthy one indeed, but not one that truly fired my imagination. The hero was too squeaky-clean, at least in Andrew's version of his life, and the enterprise was unoriginal in both conception and execution, owing far too much to Lionel Bart's hit show, *Oliver*.

33

I set to work with enormous enthusiasm, in particular for those songs that were intended to be funny. Andrew outlined the plot, played me the tunes and in many instances gave me the title as well, most of which had presumably been thought up by his ex-wordsmith school pal who had already had a go. I skipped a day at the solicitors' office, faking illness, to write my first batch of theatrical lyrics. I did not know it that day but I had changed careers.

A And even if the two of us failed to challenge the top musical composers successfully, then we could try to knock the Beatles and Rolling Stones off their perches later, in the summer. The Everly Brothers had just made a comeback and would clearly be in need of some new material.

B By then I would have surely grown out of pop music as my father had confidently predicted I would by the time I was twenty-one. This was worrying – if he was right I only had a few more months of enjoying it.

C As he confidently continued to bash out selections from some of the many shows he had written and produced at school, I was reminded of many of the best show albums from my parents' LP collection. He needed a new lyricist for the outside world.

D But it seemed to me that plenty of other blokes around my age (twenty) and not overburdened with talent were making it and I wished to be of their number. There were even guys from my home town and from public school in the pop charts – surely I had the qualifications.

E I wasn't convinced by the idea for a musical that he had been working on for the past year, but in 1965 I was rarely convinced about anything. His talent was beyond question and he claimed to have all the contacts. I was soon back in his drawing room.

F My own ambitions were just as insane as his; I wanted to be a pop star, for all the healthy reasons – women, money and fame. The difference between Andrew and myself was that my dreams were never life or death to me, though it's easy to say that now. They might have become so had I failed.

G On the other hand, Andrew's conviction of his score's precocious brilliance was infectious and not totally unjustified. What did I know about musicals? As David Land, later to be my agent for over a quarter of a century, memorably (and repeatedly) said, if there's a demand for one hamburger bar on the block, there is room for two. We could be the second hamburger joint.

H Here was the largest collection of records I had ever seen, the first stereo record player and tuner I had come across and the astonishing evidence that a teenager existed who had spent money on Georgian wine glasses, pictures and furniture.

Part 4

You are going to read an extract from a novel. For questions **34–40**, choose the answer (**A**, **B**, **C** or **D**) which you think fits best according to the text.

Mark your answers **on the separate answer sheet**.

I chose this place to live, believing I would find anonymity among those who did not care if the plaster and glass and paintwork of rented houses splintered and decayed, who were not reproached by gardens gone to seed and rotting sofas. In that hope, as in most things, I was proved wrong. People in the shops, who are living their real lives, even if you aren't, soon start to recognise you. Next door's full-blown roses pouring over the fence are persistent reminders that the gardens were loved once.

Usually, I stay inside trying to forget that there is a summer going on out there, but tonight, I am watching the swifts flying in the transparent space between the treetops and roofs. I have cut back rosemary and lemon balm to make a space for a chair and my arms and hands are tingling with stings and scratches. It is a narrow London garden, where plants must grow tall or sprawling to survive.

'Been doing a spot of clearing, I see.'

It's my upstairs neighbour, Jaz, leaning out of the window, the author of several unpublished manuscripts I am sometimes called upon to dissemble about in my capacity as an English teacher. I have a copy of the latest in my possession now.

'How's the work going, Jaz?'

'For goodness sake. In no other profession is one called on to account for oneself a thousand times a day by every Tom, Dick or Harry.' Her voice tails off, then rallies. 'Tell you what, Ann, I've got something to drink in the fridge. I'll bring it down.'

I don't want Jaz in the garden, and I see now, dully, that it looks mangled and bereft. The only access to this garden is through my flat and Jaz is banging on my door. 'So, you're on holiday now, you jammy so-and-so.' She sprawls, in shorts and vest, on the chair while I drop a cushion onto what had once been a little lawn. 'Cheers,' she says in her delusion of youth, 'I should've gone into teaching – a writer doesn't have holidays. Still, you know what they say, those who can, do, those who can't, teach.'

And there are those who can neither write nor teach.

'So, what plans for the hols?'

All my postponed dread of the school year's ending engulfs me. Empty days. Hot pavements blobbed with melting chewing gum. The walk down to the shops and back. The little park with its fountain, and loneliness sitting beside me on the bench.

'Actually, I'm going down to Stonebridge tomorrow. I've been meaning to ask you if you'd feed the cats.' My heart starts racing as I speak.

'Of course I will,' Jaz says. 'If I'm around,' knowing, as I did, that she would be. 'So where will you stay? Some bijou B and B?'

'No. I'll be staying with my oldest friend, Ruby, at the Rising Sun. We've known each other since we were eight.' It isn't true that I shall stay there, but then I spend my life dealing with fiction of one sort or another.

'Going back to your roots. So what do you think of it so far? My opus?'

My silence on the subject has forced Jaz to enquire about her manuscript, *The Cruelty of Red Vans*, which lies half-heartedly half-read on my desk.

I like the title and tell her so. I can see how red vans could be cruel, always bringing presents and mail-order goodies to other houses and delivering returned manuscripts in jiffy bags to hers. Something prompts me to speak honestly for once.

'Let me give you a little tip, dear,' I begin.

'What?' She is affronted.

'Try writing about *nice* people for a change, *pretty* people who at least *aspire* to being good: a touch less solipsism, a bit more *fiction* …'

'Teachers!' Jaz is a mutinous schoolgirl about to snatch back a poorly marked essay.

'I myself keep a journal, I have for years, in which I write down something good, however small or trivial, about each day.' My words sound as prissy as my old-fashioned print dress.

'Keep a journal! Nice people! Get a life, Ann.'

Oh, I've got a life. I've got my work, and I go out sometimes and fly home again, sitting on the tube with my nose in a book.

When at last we go inside, my calm kitchen gives a moment's reassurance, then out of the blue comes the image of my school geography teacher Miss Tarrantine, who must have been about the age I am now, closing an ancient reptilian eyelid in a monstrous wink as she tells us, 'I've had my moments.' We nearly died.

34 The place the narrator chose to live has not met her expectations because

  A residents do not look after the area.
  B she did not anticipate the difficulties of her lifestyle.
  C usual patterns of interaction have not stopped.
  D she has not found people who share her tastes.

35 What does Jaz's response to the question about her work indicate?

  A She resents being compared to a man.
  B She resents being asked it continually.
  C She understands the narrator means no harm by it.
  D She knows what reply she is expected to give.

36 From the narrator's point of view, Jaz's ability as a writer

  A mirrors her own.
  B demonstrates little potential.
  C is likely to improve with help.
  D reveals considerable talent.

37 What advice does Ann give Jaz?

  A She should be more inventive.
  B She should analyse her own situation.
  C She should read more literature.
  D She should describe people she knows.

38 How does Jaz react to what she is told?

  A She secretly recognises the value of the advice.
  B She is hostile to what she hears.
  C She resents being treated like a schoolgirl.
  D She criticises Ann's choice of profession.

39 How does Ann view her present life?

  A She appreciates its benefits.
  B She enjoys the time available for reading.
  C She knows she should go out more often.
  D She is aware of its true nature.

40 Thinking of Miss Tarrantine makes Ann

  A see an amusing side to herself.
  B realise how unattractive Miss Tarrantine was.
  C appreciate how different her life is from Miss Tarrantine's.
  D recognise how she appears to others.

PAPER 2   WRITING (2 hours)

Part 1

You **must** answer this question. Write your answer in **300–350** words in an appropriate style.

1 Your tutor has asked you to listen to the radio programme, *Dilemmas*, as part of your course on social issues and then to write an essay expressing your views on the points raised. The programme was described in a media magazine in the following way:

> 'Tonight's programme is about money. In many parts of the world people have more money than they had thirty years ago. They may have more possessions but they are not always happier. The first guest believes that money can buy happiness, but in the studio audience we may have some people who believe that it is possible to be happy without much money...'

Write your **essay**.

Part 2

Write an answer to **one** of the questions **2–5** in this part. Write your answer in **300–350** words in an appropriate style.

---

2   The editor of a magazine called *Leisure Today* has asked for letters from readers who collect things as a hobby. Readers are asked to explain what they collect, describe how they find new objects for their collections and account for the satisfaction they get from their hobby. You decide to write a letter to the magazine about your collection.

Write your **letter**. Do not write any postal addresses.

3   A publication called *The 50 Best Holiday Destinations* has invited readers to send in detailed reports of a recent holiday at any **one** destination. The report should include comments on accommodation, food, leisure facilities, places of interest and nightlife. It should also state how strongly and for what reasons the destination is recommended.

Write your **report**.

4   A popular magazine has invited readers to contribute articles to a series called *A Day That Changed My Life*. You decide to submit an article. You should describe an experience that had an important effect on you and say what the consequences were.

Write your **article**.

5   Based on your reading of **one** of these books, write on **one** of the following:

(a)   John Wyndham: *The Day of the Triffids*
You belong to a reading group. Members of the group have been asked to write reviews of novels in which they discuss the opinion that 'Science Fiction may be exciting and entertaining, although it is rarely believable.' You decide to write about *The Day of the Triffids*, referring to characters and events in the story.

Write your **review**.

(b)   Graham Greene: *Our Man in Havana*
A popular magazine has asked its readers to submit articles for a series on women in fiction. You decide to contribute by writing about Beatrice, describing her character and discussing how well she deals with the unusual circumstances she becomes involved in.

Write your **article**.

(c)   Anne Tyler: *The Accidental Tourist*
A popular literary magazine has recently featured readers' opinions about minor characters in novels. You decide to write a letter to the magazine in which you discuss the part played by Julian Edge in *The Accidental Tourist*. You should describe his character and his relationship with Rose and other members of the Leary family.

Write your **letter**. Do not write any postal addresses.

PAPER 3   USE OF ENGLISH (1 hour 30 minutes)

Part 1

For questions **1–15**, read the text below and think of the word which best fits each space. Use only **one** word in each space. There is an example at the beginning **(0)**.

Write your answers in CAPITAL LETTERS **on the separate answer sheet**.

Example: | 0 | W | I | T | H | O | U | T | | | | | | | | | | |

The ways we have changed

It is hard for almost everyone, but especially the young, to imagine a world **(0)**..*without*.. television. We have **(1)**............ to expect that all the important news of the day, worldwide, will be there **(2)**............ the touch of a button. In times **(3)**............ by, only the literate knew what was going on in the world, and **(4)**............ only after a long delay. But now it is possible for any of us to watch world events as they occur. **(5)**............ has shortened the distance that divides our private lives **(6)**............ the outside world to **(7)**............ an extent as television.

Time and **(8)**............ , television transports us to the habitats of rare animals, and we may identify **(9)**............ them. Concern for damage to the environment extends far and **(10)**............ . We worry about the influence of technology not just in our cities but on us **(11)**............ people. Increasingly, we see **(12)**............ as part of the planet **(13)**............ than in isolation.

(14)............ was once the prerogative of scholars is now accessible to countless people through the medium of television. **(15)**............ this form of popular education can be regarded as superficial, it represents a broadening of knowledge.

Part 2

For questions **16–25**, read the text below. Use the word given in capitals at the end of some of the lines to form a word that fits in the space in the same line. There is an example at the beginning **(0)**.

Write your answers in CAPITAL LETTERS **on the separate answer sheet**.

Example: | 0 | E | D | U | C | A | T | I | O | N | | | | | | |

In a class of your own

Like any form of **(0)**...*education*... , the self-taught course has its advantages as   **EDUCATE**
well as its **(16)**............ .   **DRAW**

On the one hand, you are **(17)**............ ; no classroom, no timetable and so no   **AUTONOMY**
risk of getting a bad **(18)**............ record. You are able to study at your own pace;   **ATTEND**
at home, in the car or wherever your Walkman takes you. On the other hand, can
you really trust yourself to be **(19)**............ motivated without some form of   **SUFFICE**
external stimulus?

I procrastinated **(20)**............ before beginning my first Spanish course. I made   **DREAD**
coffee, did domestic chores that were anything but **(21)**............ ; I even watched   **PRESS**
daytime television. But, once I got started, I found the course surprisingly
engaging. The multimedia formats, colourful textbooks and **(22)**............   **IMAGINE**
teaching methods all drew me into the excitement of learning a new language.

Of course, if your aim is **(23)**............ in the language, nothing can beat actually   **EXPERT**
going to the country concerned. Round-the-clock **(24)**............ is clearly always   **IMMERSE**
going to be more effective than the odd half hour with a set of tapes. But that odd
half hour will give you an **(25)**............ head start when you step out onto the   **VALUE**
streets.

Part 3

For questions **26–31**, think of **one** word only which can be used appropriately in all three sentences. Here is an example **(0)**.

Example:

0 Some of the tourists are hoping to get compensation for the poor state of the hotel, and I think they have a very .... case.

There's no point in trying to wade across the river, the current is far too ....

If you're asking me which of the candidates should get the job, I'm afraid I don't have any .... views either way.

| **0** | S | T | R | O | N | G | | | | | | | | | | | | | |

Write **only** the missing word in CAPITAL LETTERS **on the separate answer sheet**.

---

26 When Janet got down to work, every complex problem was swiftly .... to its most important points.

Everything got worse and worse and eventually he was .... to begging.

The doctor noticed that the swelling had been considerably .... by the application of the new ointment.

27 Boris had a small part in the play but .... as a programme seller before the performance.

Pippa .... her efforts as she was determined to succeed.

The investment was so good that I .... my money in three months.

28 Winning the competition came as a .... surprise to Marianne.

Robin is determined to keep on collecting football stickers until he has a .... set.

Sir Ralph arrived at the fancy-dress party in full army uniform, ... with badges and medals.

29   They heard the news of their wrecked holiday plans with .... hearts.

For anyone convicted of such a crime, there is a .... penalty.

Simon is convinced he will be able to carry that .... rucksack all the way.

30   The most expensive hotels are those which .... the sea.

As an actor he had to .... criticism from the press on a regular basis.

Cristina found it hard to .... the fact that her marriage was over.

31   When buying a house, it is always a good idea to have some money in ....
for unexpected expenses.

These fine textiles were woven by .... in India.

The newscaster reported that the situation in the capital was getting out of ....

Part 4

For questions **32–39**, complete the second sentence so that it has a similar meaning to the first sentence, using the word given. **Do not change the word given.** You must use between **three** and **eight** words, including the word given.

Here is an example **(0)**.

Example:

0 Do you mind if I watch you while you paint?

objection

Do you .... you while you paint?

0	*have any objection to my watching*

Write **only** the missing words **on the separate answer sheet**.

---

32 The manufacturing process was delayed by problems no one had foreseen.

held

The manufacturing process .... problems.

33 The only thing I could do was sit and wait.

anything

There .... sit and wait.

34 Eliza would never have got the job if her brother hadn't advised her when she completed the application form.

without

Eliza would never have got the job .... completing the application form.

35 The new cinema will be built as long as the council agrees to our plans for extra car parking space.

subject

The new cinema will be built .... to our plans for extra car parking space.

36 'My trainer's foreign accent makes it hard to follow what he says,' Sue said.

which

Sue explained to me that it .... it hard to follow what he said.

37 There are very few opportunities for Tim to play the saxophone these days.

get

Very rarely .... the saxophone these days.

38 The guide pointed out to us the magnificent carvings above the windows.

drew

The guide .... the magnificent carvings above the windows.

39 We ask passengers not to leave their seats until the aircraft doors have been opened.

remain

Passengers .... until the aircraft doors have been opened.

Part 5

For questions **40–44**, read the following texts on good and bad smells. For questions **40–43**, answer with a word or short phrase. You do not need to write complete sentences. For question **44**, write a summary according to the instructions given.

Write your answers to questions **40–44 on the separate answer sheet**.

Some years ago, a book was published called *The Romantic Story of Scent*. On the jacket, it said that since it was almost impossible to describe a fragrance in words, the readers had been given the scents themselves. Eighteen labels on the jacket flaps corresponded to the eighteen scents described – just scratch and sniff. Personally, I think the resultant conflict of odours was likely to be unbearable.   **line 4**

It is all very well saying that this sort of thing will be limited to cookery books, encyclopaedias of wild flowers and the like, but sooner or later some clown will commission a history of those hot dog stands that infest London, the stench from which is detectable a hundred metres away.

I believe that some theatrical and film producers, in a misguided attempt to add realism to the work on offer, have tried pumping the appropriate artificial smells into the auditorium, as called for by the story, only to find their plan going badly awry. In one case, they had failed to devise any means of removing each smell from the place before the next one was due, so that as the heroine was unwrapping an exquisite flower, the audience was still being regaled with the fish that had been   **line 13**
consumed in the previous scene.

40 Which **three** words in the second paragraph suggest that the writer is not in favour of 'scratch and sniff' books? (line 4)

....

41 Explain in your own words what point the writer is making in paragraph 3 with his example of 'flower' and 'fish'. (line 13)

....

Smell has the ability to bring alive memories and images more intensely than other senses, but nowadays most scents owe more to science and computers than to the mystique of   line 2
the finest perfume houses. One new company sees itself as translating ideas and concepts   line 3
into smells. Many thousands of people have been interviewed to help the company get as close as possible to what its customers want.

The problem is that it's difficult to talk about smells in a way that will mean anything to the man or woman in the street because most people are unable to communicate their feelings about smells beyond whether they like them or not. In an attempt to get round this inadequacy, the company has developed a computer program which makes visual the scent patterns of individual fragrances.

As a result, the company can measure and recreate any smell in the world. No smells are ruled out. Some smells like vanilla, chocolate and toffee were once considered bizarre perfumes, but have now become mainstream. For most people, though, the latest perfumes emerging from the most fashionable designers may prove a challenge too far: they include 'mud' and 'charcoal'.

42   How does the writer suggest that the 'mystique of the finest perfume houses' (lines 2 and 3) has been lost?

....

43   In your own words, explain what, according to the text, the key feature of the new computer program is.

....

44   In a paragraph of **50–70** words, summarise **in your own words as far as possible** the possible consequences described in **both** texts of new developments in the creation and use of artificial smells. Write your summary **on the separate answer sheet**.

PAPER 4   LISTENING (40 minutes approximately)

Part 1

You will hear four different extracts. For questions **1–8**, choose the answer (**A**, **B** or **C**) which fits best according to what you hear. There are two questions for each extract.

Extract One

You hear an expert describing how he helped to convict a criminal.

1 What is his area of expertise?

    A analysis of fibres in textiles
    B chemical components of dyes
    C patterns of wear in cloth

	1

2 How does he make a positive identification?

    A matching individual characteristics
    B referring to computer records
    C conducting chemical tests

	2

Extract Two

You hear a radio interview with a teacher who accompanies students on school trips.

3 What effect have school trips had on the teacher?

    A They have enriched her professionally.
    B She has become a more understanding parent.
    C They have increased her school responsibilities.

	3

4 She retains her teacher's role when on trips in order to

    A reassure students.
    B encourage learning.
    C maintain discipline.

	4

Extract Three

You hear a playwright being interviewed on the radio about the arts in Britain.

5 What is the playwright's view of the government's role in the arts?

    A to support the traditional arts
    B to further its own aims
    C to ensure an even distribution of resources

6 According to the playwright, the success of big musicals in the 1980s led to

    A a serious decline in the high arts.
    B the virtual collapse of the radical theatre.
    C a dialogue between classical and popular music.

Extract Four

You hear twin sisters from an Asian background discussing a British television programme about twins.

7 What did the first twin dislike about the programme?

    A It spent too much time on the scientific aspects.
    B It was over-complex for the average viewer.
    C It focused on the negative aspects of being a twin.

8 The second twin believes that people in western cultures

    A overvalue individuality.
    B expect twins to look identical.
    C assume twins have similar traits.

Part 2

You will hear a talk given by a naturalist who is interested in a type of insect called the damselfly. For questions **9–17**, complete the sentences with a word or short phrase.

There is a lack of information about both the number and

	9

of damselflies across different locations in Britain.

The damselfly has been badly affected by recent changes in the countryside, for example,

	10

and the filling-in of ponds.

An observer can identify a damselfly by the position of its

	11

while it is resting.

Because of their colours, some damselflies are described as resembling types of

	12

The commonest species of damselfly in the speaker's area is called the

	13

The most endangered species of damselfly in the speaker's area is called the

	14

The best place to find damselflies is near water which is

	15

, and which supports plant life.

Damselflies are easiest to see in the hours immediately following

	16

The Conservation Trust would like to make a

	17

of places where damselflies can still be found.

Part 3

You will hear a radio interview with the artist, Madeline Knowles. For questions **18–22**, choose the answer (**A**, **B**, **C** or **D**) which fits best according to what you hear.

---

18 What motivates Madeline in her choice of subject?

  A a desire to produce beautiful paintings
  B a rejection of the unpleasantness of life
  C an appreciation of essential qualities
  D a search for her own inner peace

  18

19 What, in Madeline's view, is the relationship between artists and the world they live in?

  A They want to reveal the patterns in life.
  B They value the supernatural element in art.
  C They have to provide what people want.
  D They have difficulty in communicating with people.

  19

20 Why did Madeline first take up painting?

  A It had been a secret ambition of hers to paint.
  B A change of focus was required in her teaching.
  C Her students requested help with their painting.
  D She saw it as a fulfilling way of expressing herself.

  20

21 How was the rock star influenced by seeing Madeline's painting of a path?

  A He was inspired to paint his first picture.
  B He commissioned her to paint a picture of his house.
  C He wanted to introduce a similar feature into his garden.
  D He became interested in a new style of painting.

  21

22 How does Madeline help the rock star with his painting?

  A by providing him with technical tips
  B by discussing his involvement with the subject
  C by suggesting suitable subjects to paint
  D by offering advice on painting the countryside

  22

Part 4

You will hear a discussion on the radio on the subject of rock festivals. For questions **23–28**, decide whether the opinions are expressed by only one of the speakers, or whether the speakers agree.

Write **T** for Tim,
       M for Maria,
or   **B** for Both, where they agree.

---

23   Too many people travel to rock festivals by car. | 23 |

24   Rock festivals in cities cause more problems than those in the countryside. | 24 |

25   The problem at the Tandem Festival could have been anticipated. | 25 |

26   There are sometimes ugly structures left after festivals have taken place. | 26 |

27   At Greenwood, there is now a greater concern about removing waste. | 27 |

28   Festivals are held in order to make a profit for the organisers. | 28 |

PAPER 5   SPEAKING (19 minutes)

There are two examiners. One (the Interlocutor) conducts the test, providing you with the necessary materials and explaining what you have to do. The other examiner (the Assessor) will be introduced to you, but then takes no further part in the interaction.

Part 1 (3 minutes)

The Interlocutor first asks you and your partner a few questions which focus on information about yourselves and personal opinions.

Part 2 (4 minutes)

In this part of the test you and your partner are asked to talk together. The Interlocutor places a set of pictures on the table in front of you. This stimulus provides the basis for a discussion. The Interlocutor first asks an introductory question which focuses on one or two of the pictures. After about a minute, the Interlocutor gives you both a decision-making task based on the same set of pictures.

The picture for Part 2 is on page C3 of the colour section.

Part 3 (12 minutes)

You are each given the opportunity to talk for two minutes, to comment after your partner has spoken and to take part in a more general discussion.

The Interlocutor gives you a card with a question written on it and asks you to talk about it for two minutes. After you have spoken, your partner is first asked to comment and then the Interlocutor asks you both another question related to the topic on the card. This procedure is repeated, so that your partner receives a card and speaks for two minutes, you are given an opportunity to comment and a follow-up question is asked.

Finally, the Interlocutor asks some further questions, which leads to a discussion on a general theme related to the subjects already covered in Part 3.

The cards for Part 3 are on pages C2 and C10 of the colour section.

Test 2

PAPER 1 READING (1 hour 30 minutes)

Part 1

For questions **1–18**, read the three texts below and decide which answer (**A**, **B**, **C** or **D**) best fits each gap.

Mark your answers **on the separate answer sheet**.

Paul Simon

Rock and roll in the 1950s was primarily a youth cult, but its lasting importance **(1)** .... in the seismic impact it had on the middle class and the middle-aged. It also **(2)** .... the way for the next generation of rock idols, who listened to it awestruck and aware that this strange, unsettling sound would somehow, irrevocably, be **(3)** .... with their destinies.

For Paul Simon, as for other youngsters in the US, the chief **(4)** .... for hearing this new and invigorating type of music that was sweeping the country was courtesy of Alan Freed's radio show, *Moondog Rock 'n' Roll Party*. Freed's show was **(5)** .... listening for a whole generation of fledgling rock idols. Like the young John Lennon, 3,000 miles away in Liverpool, with his ear **(6)** .... to Radio Luxembourg – the only European outlet for the new rock and roll – Paul Simon was fascinated by the sounds pouring from Freed's show, and prepared himself for the next big step for a rock and roll obsessed teenager, the switch from listening to others' music to making his own.

1 A stood	**B** stayed	**C** held	**D** lay
2 A paved	**B** fashioned	**C** generated	**D** grounded
3 A fastened	**B** joined	**C** linked	**D** related
4 A opportunity	**B** chance	**C** way	**D** access
5 A needed	**B** obliged	**C** demanded	**D** required
6 A engrossed	**B** glued	**C** sealed	**D** enthralled

Snow

No path was visible, but I thought that I would be all right if I walked with due caution. The wind hammered down from the heights, knocking me over as I slid and **(7)** ..... on the slippery ice. Suddenly the innocent-looking snow **(8)** ..... way beneath me. I dropped, startled, into a hole some four feet deep. The snow had formed a roof over the gap between two rocks, melting away to leave nothing but a thin **(9)** .... through which I had plunged. I **(10)** .... myself out, shaken and unnerved, wondering what I would have done if the hole had been thirty feet deep. I sat back against the top of a pine tree that protruded from the snow to take **(11)** .... of the situation. In an hour I had covered about half a mile. It was perfectly clear that I would have to **(12)** .... my plan.

7	**A** slithered	**B** swooped	**C** skipped	**D** swept
8	**A** sank	**B** gave	**C** opened	**D** fell
9	**A** lining	**B** fabric	**C** crust	**D** cloak
10	**A** hauled	**B** handed	**C** carted	**D** trailed
11	**A** issue	**B** thought	**C** stock	**D** gist
12	**A** abandon	**B** neglect	**C** desist	**D** refute

Qualitative Research

There are now numerous books which attempt to give guidance to researchers about qualitative research. While much has been written about the collection of data, the books are often **(13)** .... about the processes and procedures associated with data analysis. Indeed, much mystery surrounds the way researchers analyse their data. **(14)** ...., we invited a range of social scientists who have **(15)** .... in qualitative projects to discuss the **(16)** .... that they used. The idea was to share insight and understanding of the process of qualitative data analysis rather than to produce a guidebook for the intending researcher. Such a task involves a process of demystification, of **(17)** .... implicit procedures more explicit. While this may sound straightforward, we have found it far from simple. We have therefore given our contributors the opportunity to **(18)** .... their work in a range of styles, which include autobiographical narratives and more impersonal forms.

13	**A** silent	**B** dark	**C** blank	**D** dumb
14	**A** However	**B** Accordingly	**C** Even so	**D** In essence
15	**A** employed	**B** engaged	**C** exploited	**D** entered
16	**A** accounts	**B** manners	**C** approaches	**D** modes
17	**A** turning	**B** making	**C** putting	**D** getting
18	**A** propose	**B** render	**C** extend	**D** present

Part 2

You are going to read four extracts which are all concerned in some way with writing. For questions **19–26**, choose the answer (**A**, **B**, **C** or **D**) which you think fits best according to the text.

Mark your answers **on the separate answer sheet**.

Self-help books

Diane Reverend was a mere editor at Random House in New York when she first saw a manuscript by an unknown pop psychologist, Dr John Gray. 'I took one look at the title and knew it would be a number one bestseller,' she says, chuckling, and she was right. The desperately understanding Dr Gray is now a multimillionaire and Diane Reverend has her own company. Dr Gray's slim volume on how to bridge communication gaps between the sexes is the unofficial mascot of a huge and expanding self-help industry that may, as its insiders claim, answer some of Americans' myriad yearnings for betterment. It also feeds off those yearnings, creates hundreds more and – not incidentally –   **line 9** props up the entire world of New York publishing.

As Britain is learning, the genre can fill entire walls with tomes as quackish and histrionic as their covers – but there are worse. For every self-help title published, thousands are rejected as too derivative or specialised. This is no   **line 13** small mercy. As a new breed of heavyweight editor-cum-agent goes looking for the next lightweight blockbuster, prose style is the last thing on anybody's mind. Marketability is everything. 'How promotable is the author? What's the "hook"? Is it universal enough?' Ms Reverend rattles off the key questions, then admits: 'If someone comes to me with a really catchy title, that's two thirds of the battle won. You know you can reach people.'

19 What is the writer suggesting by his use of the phrase 'not incidentally' (line 9)?

    A that the success of Dr Gray's book took other publishers by surprise
    B that a major attraction of self-help books to publishers is financial gain
    C that self-help books do not really help readers to feel better
    D that publishers outside New York would not have started the self-help industry

20 What, according to the writer, is 'no small mercy' (lines 13–14)?

    A the number of self-help books that are being published
    B the decision whether to publish certain self-help books
    C the importance attached to self-help books as a genre
    D the fact that some self-help books do not get published

Autobiographies

There has to be a tacit understanding, a pact, between an autobiographer and reader that the truth is being told. Such a pact is, I would guess, rarely observed to the full. There are many reasons why the writer should lapse. There may be actions or thoughts which he feels it is simply too shameful to make public. There may be things he decides against putting down on paper because (as he rationalises) they are not important enough. There are also more complex and interesting reasons for surreptitiously breaking the pact. The autobiographer may decide that the ultimate goal of the work, the truth about himself, can be served by inventing stories that encapsulate the truth more neatly, more pointedly, than strict adherence to the facts ever could. Or he may break the pact by deciding, from the beginning, never to adhere to it. He may call his book an autobiography simply in order to create a positive balance of credulity in the reader's mind that will be extremely convenient for him in his storytelling, and which, in the case of his more naive readers, may not be exhausted even by the time the story ends, so that these readers will go away thinking they have read a true history, when they have read nothing but a fiction. All of which can be done in no particular spirit of cynicism.

21   The writer states that some autobiographers who break the 'pact' with readers do so because

   A   they have a very low regard for their readers.
   B   they feel this enables them to create a more accurate impression.
   C   they fear they cannot describe real events entertainingly.
   D   they are simply unaware of the fact that they are doing so.

22   What does 'All of which' (in the last sentence) refer to?

   A   the types of pact between writer and reader
   B   ways of deceiving the more naive readers
   C   ways of breaking the pact
   D   the reasons for disguising fiction or truth

Dashiell Hammett's detective stories

Students of the detective story have explained the flourishing of this genre as an expression of the conflicts of late nineteenth and early twentieth century society. The detective story is essentially an allegory. The crime is a symbolic enactment of some innate human impulse of lust or greed, and its solution, at least in the traditional story, represents the reintegration of the personality with society, its lawless impulses quelled so that society can again function smoothly. In Hammett's peculiar version, society is returned to its former state, but that itself is shown to be corrupt and false.

The hunter and the hunted in Hammett's tales are two aspects of the same personality. The private eye and his prey understand each other and are, in a strange way, comfortable with each other. The private eye has a foot in each camp. From the point of view of the criminal he is a bit too straight, and from that of the law a bit too seedy. He is at once a crook and a competitor. The mission of the private eye is sometimes tempered by his sense of complicity, and sometimes his punitive zeal is intensified by his anxiety about this ambiguity.

23   The writer describes Hammett's detective stories as 'peculiar' because

    A   they do not conform to the theory that detective stories are allegories.
    B   they are not resolved in the way that other detective stories are.
    C   they are based on a particularly negative view of human nature.
    D   they present an unconventional view as to why crimes are committed.

24   Which of the following does the writer consider to be ambiguous?

    A   the private eye's position in society
    B   the criminal's position in society
    C   the attitude of the criminal towards the private eye
    D   the attitude of the law towards the private eye

SCIENCE WRITING

Today's greatest scientific essayist is Stephen Jay Gould. To discuss that art and hear his advice, I met him in an unfamiliar milieu: at the Grand Hotel (where he was staying while promoting his new book). Neither of us, it has to be said, felt much at home. As for writing a piece set in surroundings of such lifeless self-aggrandisement, Gould said: 'I couldn't do it: Trollope might but he knew the culture. And knowing the culture is central to being a successful writer. Science, for example, is a civilisation of its own. As a result, only scientists can make a good job of presenting it. If you don't live in the community and don't understand its rules, you are crippled from the start.'

One of Gould's axioms is: never write down to the reader. 'Make no   line 11
concessions,' he says. 'You can simplify the language but must never adulterate it. Above all, you cannot simplify the argument. Once readers notice that they are being patronised, your piece is dead.'

25 Which of the following do we learn about the Grand Hotel?

   A   It inspired Gould to talk about the role of the science writer in society.
   B   Another writer had described the atmosphere there very well.
   C   The writer of this article thought it an unappealing place.
   D   It made Gould aware that the experience of many science writers is too narrow.

26 Who is Gould talking about when he mentions 'the community' (line 11)?

   A   scientists
   B   ordinary people
   C   science writers
   D   highly educated people

Part 3

You are going to read an introduction to a book. Seven paragraphs have been removed from the extract. Choose from the paragraphs **A–H** the one which fits each gap (**27–33**). There is one extra paragraph which you do not need to use.

Mark your answers **on the separate answer sheet**.

Advertising on trial

If you work for an advertising agency, the early years of the 1990s may well have been the toughest of your professional life. The recession in business was bad enough. It was longer, deeper and more severe than anticipated by even the most pessimistic, hitting industrialised nations as hard as anything else for thirty years.

27	

Every single business in the country was affected, some – the vehicle and building trades – finding themselves 30 per cent down. A lot of people – a lot of companies – in a lot of countries suffered. Of course, advertising people are scarcely unique in losing their jobs in such difficult times, but of all those still in employment, they often feel particularly under pressure.

28	

And yet, alongside these psychological and financial imperatives lies an almost paradoxical rise in the perceived importance of the marketing process. The notion that companies should be making sure they are producing services and goods that their customers want, as opposed to merely what it is convenient for them to provide, is not a new one. Still, it's scarcely unfair to say that it has been only over the past ten or fifteen years that many companies seem to have put the idea intentionally, rather than fortuitously, into practice.

29	

All these things have pleasingly increased the status of marketing people, while simultaneously adding to their burden. Marketing is increasingly regarded as that which it is not: a universal panacea. With approximately half of most marketing budgets being

spent on advertising, there's some truth in saying that the buck then stops with the ad-people. It is certainly true that if the 80s was the decade in which advertising never had it so good, the start of the 90s saw the industry enduring its worst downturn for a generation. This was, of course, partly a direct consequence of the economic climate at the time.

30	

And, generally, in the absence of concrete, convincing and quantitative evidence to the contrary, they had to conclude that the benefits of advertising might be questionable. At a time when enthusiasm to account for every dollar spent was naturally high, it was simply not clear enough to many client companies exactly what they were getting for the large sums of money they were spending, exactly what return they were seeing on their investment. Advertising – ever a business to excite the suspicions of the sceptic – was, as a consequence, more than ever before on trial.

31	

Now, while none of this should elicit sympathy for a thoroughly tough business, it does mean that many of those advertising people still in work continue to face precisely the same problems as their clients: how to do more with less. If this is, in itself, sufficiently trying, a number of other factors have made the production of effective advertising particularly difficult.

32	

These include, for example, the dramatic demographic changes facing much of the West; the burgeoning power of the retailer; the changing needs and desires of consumers; the rise of sponsorship;

the increasingly onerous legal restrictions on advertising. And, of course, for some companies there is the new challenge of advertising abroad. Together with the economic situation, it is these matters which have forced many of those responsible for advertising to revisit Lord Leverhulme's commonplace that: 'Only half my advertising works. The trouble is I don't know which half.' Because now more than ever before, the pressure is on to increase the proportion of advertising that works.

This means that while conferences and seminars may provide some useful information, the books currently available on advertising, and how to do it, really don't. Those that are available tend to treat the process of producing advertising with too much respect. To give the impression that the work advertising agencies produce is invariably of the highest quality, deeply considered and remarkable value for money, is neither true nor likely to help those employees of the client company who are ultimately responsible.

33

A Thus, client companies almost everywhere took the view of one of their leaders quoted in the British trade magazine *Campaign*: 'We want better strategies, better targeting, better creativity, better media placement, better thinking. We aim to ensure we get advertising agencies' best people on our business and then ensure they are motivated to work their fingers to the bone, producing outstanding work for us.'

B The consequences have been that marketing activities have at last begun to be given the attention they deserve by management, that these people have acquired a little learning about the subject, and that a few brands have actually begun to be genuinely marketed.

C Ultimately, the poverty of the current advertising scene is due to the nature of the relationship between agencies and their clients. The best way of getting better advertising lies partly in improving this, and partly in adopting a more empirical approach to the whole advertising process.

D However, there was also evidence of more deep-seated change which would not simply be waved away as, and when, economic prospects brightened. The fact was that while this recession naturally caused potential clients to review, reconsider and often cut their budgets at the time, it also made them examine more closely than ever before the economics of advertising.

E It is not terribly surprising that, at the moment, help for those who want or need to do just that is far from freely available. Generally, companies and the advertising agencies they use have been far too busy simply coping with these circumstances to wish to talk or write about them, while those that have succeeded in keeping their heads above water are often understandably anxious to keep the secrets of their success to themselves.

F Seen, as they are, to spearhead efforts to support the bottom line, they suppose themselves to be under close enough scrutiny from their colleagues, let alone their bosses. Moreover, they are also faced with the very considerable problem of increasingly being asked to do their ever more difficult jobs with smaller and smaller budgets. They have been told that less must be more.

G Some of these are a direct consequence of the recession discussed earlier: the controversy over production costs, and the disinclination to take the sort of risks that are ironically often the essence of good advertising. Other events would have happened irrespective of local or global economic conditions.

H In Britain, it meant in 1991 alone that while gross domestic product (GDP) declined, interest rates remained punitively high, consumer spending on almost everything other than staples fell, more than half a million people lost their jobs, and some 75,000 homes were repossessed.

Part 4

You are going to read an extract from a novel. For questions **34–40**, choose the answer (**A**, **B**, **C** or **D**) which you think fits best according to the text.

Mark your answers **on the separate answer sheet**.

Ralph unlocked the door to his flat and as he entered the dark, motionless hall experienced that momentary qualm of ownership which even after three years still lightly besieged him sometimes when he returned alone at the end of the day. When he had first bought the flat, he used to come home in an eager, questioning mood – often as early as he could – wondering what it had been doing during the hours he had been away. It had represented a form of welcome to him, a region in which his focus was undisputed and reliable. He supposed that he should have worried about intruders or burst drains in that moment of reunion, but his flat had always been sitting waiting for him with an expression of independence or of neglect, depending on whether he'd left it tidy or not. In the end he had begun to regard it merely as another cloistered annexe of himself, a space into which the stuffy chambers of his heart and head had gradually overspilled their contents.

He had grown impatient with its inability to be transformed. There was, of course, the small, angular puddle of letters which sometimes gathered by the door and the red eye of the answering machine which could occasionally be found resuscitated and blinking with life when he returned. And he was grateful that the glassy eyes of his windows hadn't been smashed nor the contents ravished with violence, mind you, he wondered what the flat would look like afterwards.

From the dreary distance of his shabby third-floor office on the Holloway Road, Ralph often looked forward to his three or four solitary evenings at home each week. Once he had fled the fabricated world of the office and felt the memory of himself begin patchily to return on his bus journey home, he no longer needed to be on his own, a fact which seemed continually to elude him in his social calculations. Sitting exposed at his desk he would crave isolation, unlimited time alone amongst his possessions, but the relief of escape drained him and he would vainly wait for some sense of selfhood to return. Instead, there was merely a resounding emptiness, which made him suspect during his long hours of loneliness that the alien exercise of doing work which did not suit him had forced him to change, moving him further and further from what he liked to think of as himself. He would often read or listen to music as the night deepened outside, familiar habits which now, however, he would find himself asking for whom or what he did them. His points of reference had grown dim, his signposts muddied: sensations and ideas would arrive and then get lost, circulating around the junctions of his mind, unable to find a connection.

There had been a time, he supposed, when he had not felt this powerless, when, had he but perceived his own worth, he might have escaped; but he had been so eager to fix himself up with something that he had been swept along by this great desire for something, and he had followed the first course which presented itself as if it had been ordained that he should do so.

He had tried, of course, after he left university, to formulate some plan for his own betterment, but it hadn't really surprised him to find, when he searched himself for ambition, merely the desire unobtrusively to survive. He had applied for the types of jobs which had become familiar to him through the talk of his peers, had latched himself wearily on to their futures and jogged behind as they rushed towards them, unable to imagine that he might be put to some use which would manufacture as its by-product his own happiness.

He had attended his only interview gratefully, and in the fever of examination did not think to test the position – an inexplicit editorial role on a free local newspaper – for its own merits. Relieved at having pulled off twenty minutes of pleasant conversation with Neil, his boss, he had not considered the future of lengthy encounters by which he was now daily assaulted. Neil had offered him the job there and then, telling him he was the only graduate who had applied; a revelation which at the time Ralph had obscurely taken as a compliment.

34   What do we learn in the first paragraph about Ralph's current attitude towards his flat?

   A   He resents the responsibilities ownership of it involves.
   B   He regrets that he cannot put more effort into its upkeep.
   C   He is aware that he has imposed his personality on it.
   D   He sees it as an area over which he has supreme authority.

35   What do we learn from Ralph's thoughts about his answering machine?

   A   He takes some comfort from its presence.
   B   He dislikes its intrusive nature.
   C   It increases his feelings of isolation.
   D   It contributes to his sense of security.

36   According to the author, Ralph's desire to be alone is

   A   self-indulgent.
   B   conceited.
   C   self-destructive.
   D   misguided.

37   Ralph suspects that his work

   A   has restricted his other interests.
   B   should be a more sociable experience.
   C   is too complex for his limited abilities.
   D   has had a negative effect on his personality.

38   Ralph's initial concern after university had been to

   A   improve his future prospects.
   B   keep sight of his long-term goals.
   C   avoid any early mistakes.
   D   follow his own interests.

39   What approach did Ralph take in looking for a job?

   A   He tried to apply faster than other applicants.
   B   He unthinkingly adopted the ideas of others.
   C   He rehearsed for interviews with his friends.
   D   He focused on areas in which he had some experience.

40   What do we learn about Ralph's interview with Neil?

   A   Neil took pains to make Ralph feel relaxed.
   B   Ralph failed to find out about the job concerned.
   C   It was much shorter than Ralph had expected.
   D   The two men shared similar educational backgrounds.

PAPER 2 WRITING (2 hours)

Part 1

You **must** answer this question. Write your answer in **300–350** words in an appropriate style.

1 The extract below is from a letter which appeared in a national newspaper. You decide to write a reply. In your letter, respond to the issues raised and express your own opinions.

> Dear Editor,
> These days many parents give their children the freedom to make their own decisions from a very early age. They argue that this freedom helps children to learn from their mistakes and gives them the maturity and confidence to deal with the responsibilities of adult life. I don't agree. It is totally irresponsible to let young people make their own choices about friendship, leisure activities and, later on, vital decisions about their future lives.

Write your **letter**. Do not write any postal addresses.

Part 2

Write an answer to **one** of the questions **2–5** in this part. Write your answer in **300–350** words in an appropriate style.

---

2   Your course tutor has asked you to write a review of a popular soap opera which you know well, and to explain the popularity of such programmes in general.

Write your **review**.

3   Write an article for your college magazine, briefly describing a museum or exhibition that you have visited recently. Choose one exhibit which particularly impressed you, and give reasons for your choice.

Write your **article**.

4   You work for a local environmental organisation which is concerned about the effect that mass tourism is having on your region. Your manager has asked you to write a proposal in which you suggest ways of encouraging tourists to continue visiting your area without threatening the local environment.

Write your **proposal**.

5   Based on your reading of **one** of these books, write on **one** of the following:

(a)   John Wyndham: *The Day of the Triffids*
A local radio station has asked listeners to send in reports on books which they consider suitable for reading aloud on the radio. You decide to write about *The Day of the Triffids*. In your report you should consider and discuss the following two areas: episodes which contribute to the excitement of the story and relationships which add interest to the story line.

Write your **report**.

(b)   Graham Greene: *Our Man in Havana*
A literary magazine is planning a series of articles on the development of relationships in English novels. You decide to submit an article on *Our Man in Havana* in which you describe the circumstances which lead to the meeting between Wormold and Beatrice Severn, and examine the different aspects of their characters which attract them to each other.

Write your **article**.

(c)   Anne Tyler: *The Accidental Tourist*
'It occurred to him that the world was sharply divided down the middle. Some lived careful lives, and some lived careless lives.' Write an essay for your tutor discussing how far you think this view applies to Macon and Muriel, and whether you think their attitudes to life change during the course of the story.

Write your **essay**.

PAPER 3   USE OF ENGLISH (1 hour 30 minutes)

Part 1

For questions **1–15**, read the text below and think of the word which best fits each space. Use only **one** word in each space. There is an example at the beginning **(0)**.

Write your answers in CAPITAL LETTERS **on the separate answer sheet**.

Example: | **0** | *O* | F | | | | | | | | | | | | | | | |

Louis Pasteur (1822–1895)

Of the legions **(0)**....*of*..... twentieth century scientists, only a handful won worldwide recognition. Even **(1)**............ have won the greatest prize of all, the Nobel Prize, and rarer still are those who have won two. So **(2)**............ , only three people have succeeded in achieving this, but there is one scientist whose achievements would have merited four at the **(3)**............ least. **(4)**............ he died a few years **(5)**............ soon to receive the first Nobel Prize, Louis Pasteur is arguably the most celebrated of any scientist, **(6)**............ name appearing **(7)**............ countless products in homes, shops and supermarkets **(8)**............ this day.

Pioneer scientist, conqueror of disease and saviour of industries, Pasteur combined soaring intellectual powers **(9)**............ down-to-earth pragmatism, a combination which allowed him, to **(10)**............ intents and purposes, to dispose of centuries of pseudo-science. In the year 1822 when he was born, the life sciences were based on **(11)**............ more than medieval fairy tales. The underlying causes of many diseases were quite unknown. What explanations **(12)**............ exist were utterly bizarre. For instance, malaria was said to have **(13)**............ origins in 'miasmas' emanating from swamps, whereas influenza was linked to the 'influence' of celestial events, **(14)**............ as the passage of comets. Pasteur exploded **(15)**............ and many other myths.

Part 2

For questions **16–25**, read the text below. Use the word given in capitals at the end of some of the lines to form a word that fits in the space in the same line. There is an example at the beginning **(0)**.

Write your answers in CAPITAL LETTERS **on the separate answer sheet**.

Example: 0 C O M P A R A T I V E L Y

Rain making

When it rains, it doesn't always pour. During a typical storm, a **(0)**.*comparatively*.   **COMPARE**

small amount of the locked up moisture in each cloud reaches the ground as rain.

So the idea that human **(16)**............ – a rain dance, perhaps – might encourage   **INTERVENE**

the sky to give up a little **(17)**............ water has been around since prehistoric   **ADD**

times. More recently, would-be rain makers have used a more direct

(18)............ – that of throwing various chemicals out of aeroplanes in an effort   **PROCEED**

to wring more rain from the clouds, a practice known as 'cloud seeding'.

Yet such techniques, which were first developed in the 1940s, are **(19)**............   **NOTORIETY**

difficult to evaluate. It is hard to **(20)**............ , for example, how much rain would   **CERTAIN**

have fallen anyway. So, despite much anecdotal evidence of the advantages of

cloud seeding, which has led to its adoption in more than 40 countries around

the world, as far as scientists are concerned, results are still **(21)**............ . That   **CONCLUSIVE**

could be about to change. For the past three years **(22)**............ have been   **RESEARCH**

carrying out the most extensive and **(23)**............ evaluation to date of a   **RIGOUR**

revolutionary new technique which will substantially boost the volume of

(24)............ .   **RAIN**

The preliminary **(25)**............ of their experiments indicate that solid evidence   **FIND**

of the technique's effectiveness is now within the scientists' grasp.

Part 3

For questions **26–31**, think of **one** word only which can be used appropriately in all three sentences. Here is an example **(0)**.

Example:

0 Some of the tourists are hoping to get compensation for the poor state of the hotel, and I think they have a very .... case.

There's no point in trying to wade across the river, the current is far too ....

If you're asking me which of the candidates should get the job, I'm afraid I don't have any .... views either way.

0	S	T	R	O	N	G												

Write **only** the missing word in CAPITAL LETTERS **on the separate answer sheet**.

---

26 It is often said that children learn best by ....

The new sofa looked quite expensive, but in fact it was made of .... leather.

Alison could do an almost perfect .... of their teacher, and she always made everyone laugh.

27 The instructions say you should .... the glue to a slightly damp surface.

Jane will need to .... herself more to her work, if she is to get a good degree.

I've read the warning but I don't know who it can .... to.

28 When I was at university, I lived for one .... in a room which overlooked the river.

When the .... 'British Sign Language' is used, it can only refer to the signs used in the British system.

The wrongdoer was fined and sentenced to a .... of imprisonment, which many considered excessive.

29   It's a ……………………… instinct, surely, to save others, especially a child.

His ambition from adolescence was to become a ……………………… rights lawyer.

The writers which interest me most are those whose novels explore the strengths and weaknesses of ……………………… nature.

30   Following the accident, the company has agreed to carry out a thorough ……………………… of its safety procedures.

The whole policy of allowing members to borrow the club's equipment is now under ……………………… .

Sally was thrilled to see a positive ……………………… of her first novel in the local newspaper.

31   After a while, the rain became so heavy that we were forced to ……………………… shelter.

Mr Williams moved to London to ……………………… his fortune.

To climb this mountain, you must first ……………………… permission from the appropriate government department.

Part 4

For questions **32–39**, complete the second sentence so that it has a similar meaning to the first sentence, using the word given. **Do not change the word given.** You must use between **three** and **eight** words, including the word given.

Here is an example **(0)**.

Example:

0 Do you mind if I watch you while you paint?

objection

Do you .... you while you paint?

0	*have any objection to my watching*

Write **only** the missing words **on the separate answer sheet**.

---

32 Chess is a much more skilful game than backgammon.

deal

Playing chess requires .... playing backgammon.

33 John's comments on the new film were not well received.

go

John's comments on the new film .... well.

34 It was never explained why Gregor decided to leave.

given

No .... of Gregor's decision to leave.

35 Nobody expected Lucy to resign.

came

Lucy's ……………………………………………………………… everyone.

36 I was just about to leave the house when I heard the phone ring.

verge

I was ………………………………………………………… the house when I heard the phone ring.

37 Stefano decided to stay on at the hotel for two more weeks.

extend

Stefano decided ……………………………………………………… two weeks.

38 I'm sorry, I didn't mean to interrupt the meeting.

intention

I'm sorry, I ……………………………………………………… the meeting.

39 I wonder what's happened to Hans; he's normally on time for an important meeting.

unlike

I wonder what's happened to Hans; it's most …………………………………………………… for an important meeting.

Part 5

For questions **40–44**, read the following texts on fairy tales. For questions **40–43**, answer with a word or short phrase. You do not need to write complete sentences. For question **44**, write a summary according to the instructions given.

Write your answers to questions **40–44 on the separate answer sheet**.

A characteristic of many traditional tales is that they are unbelievable. For example, European fairy tales are seldom tales about fairies, although they do contain a supernatural element that is clearly imaginary. The hero or heroine is almost invariably a young person who is suffering in some way. They, and all the other characters, are stock figures. They are either altogether good or altogether bad.

The stories describe events that took place when a different range of possibilities operated at an unidentified time, long, long ago, and this is part of their attraction. The stories would, paradoxically, not be believable if the period in which they took **line 8** place was specified, or the place where they occurred was named. Wonders may take place without remark but a sharp eye is kept on practical details. It will be noticed that traditional stories are seldom soft or sentimental. The virtues which get rewarded are presence of mind, kindliness, willingness to take advice, and courage. The rewards sought after are the familiar ones: wealth, comfortable living, and an ideal partner.

Indeed, some details that appear to us romantic today may merely reflect the social conditions when the tales were formulated. When lives were short, girls of distinction married early; Sleeping Beauty, who marries her prince when sixteen (if the hundred years she has been asleep are not counted), was simply conforming to the practice of the time.

40 Which phrase in the first paragraph means 'stereotypes'?

  ....

41 Explain in your own words the paradox referred to in line 8.

  ....

There is a widespread refusal to let children know that the source of much that goes wrong in life is due to our very own natures – the propensity of all human beings for acting aggressively and selfishly. Instead we want our children to believe that, inherently, all people are good. But children know that they themselves are not always good; and often even when they are, they would prefer not to be. This contradicts what they are told by their parents and therefore makes the child a monster in his or her own eyes.

line 7

The dominant culture wishes to pretend, particularly where children are concerned, that the dark side of human beings does not exist. Psychoanalysis is viewed as having the purpose of making life easy – but this is not what Freud, its founder, intended. Psychoanalysis was created to enable people to accept the problematic nature of life without being defeated by it. Freud's prescription is that only by struggling courageously against what seem like overwhelming odds can people succeed in wringing meaning out of their existence.

line 8

This is exactly the message that fairy tales get across to the child in manifold forms: that a struggle against severe difficulties in life is unavoidable, is an intrinsic part of human existence – but that if one does not shy away, but steadfastly meets unexpected and often unjust hardships, one can master all obstacles and emerge victorious.

42 Explain in your own words why the writer states that a child may appear to be a 'monster in his or her own eyes'. (line 7)

....

43 In your own words, explain what the phrase 'The dominant culture' (line 8) refers to in the text.

....

44 In a paragraph of **50–70** words, summarise **in your own words as far as possible** how **both** texts suggest that fairy tales contain elements of real life. Write your summary **on the separate answer sheet**.

PAPER 4   LISTENING (40 minutes approximately)

Part 1

You will hear four different extracts. For questions **1–8**, choose the answer (**A**, **B** or **C**) which fits best according to what you hear. There are two questions for each extract.

Extract One

You hear a woman talking about the English language.

1 In which field does the speaker have direct experience?

   A   radio journalism
   B   newspaper editing
   C   television production

1

2 What is her attitude towards those who complain about falling standards of English?

   A   She is dismissive of their concerns.
   B   She is annoyed by their ignorance.
   C   She respects their persistence.

2

Extract Two

You hear part of an interview with a former ice skater who now dances in musical shows.

3 According to the former ice skater, the thrill of theatre work comes from

   A   the association with big-name shows.
   B   the rapport with the audience.
   C   the size of the stage.

3

4 When the former ice skater started dancing,

   A   he benefited from the support of the cast.
   B   he missed the exhilaration of speed.
   C   he learnt new ways to control his movements.

4

Extract Three

You hear a critic reviewing a new film based on a novel.

5 In the critic's opinion, the film fails because the source material was

    A dated.
    B too literary.
    C rather intellectual.

	5

6 The critic feels the two main roles

    A have become uninspiring.
    B have been made into comic figures.
    C should have been played by other actors.

	6

Extract Four

You hear part of an interview about routines with Dr Brown, a psychologist.

7 According to Dr Brown, particular routines can be beneficial because they can help people to

    A work at their own pace.
    B save time and energy.
    C cope better with changes.

	7

8 According to Dr Brown, what helps when introducing changes in the workplace?

    A decisive management
    B financial incentives
    C prior consultation

	8

Part 2

You will hear part of a radio programme about creatures which live in the sea. This part of the programme is about sponges. For questions **9–17**, complete the sentences with a word or short phrase.

GENERAL CHARACTERISTICS OF SPONGES

The speaker says that people often fail to realise the range of

| | **9** | found amongst sponges.

The speaker mentions that one of the largest sponges has the appearance of a

| | **10**

The ability of sponges to regenerate tissue means that

| | **11** | is possible.

SPONGES ON DISPLAY IN THE NATURAL HISTORY MUSEUM

What distinguishes the sponges in boxes in the museum basement is that they are all

| | **12**

The speaker says that 'glass' sponges are similar to a

| | **13** | in shape.

The shrimps found inside certain sponges are sometimes seen as symbolising both

| | **14**

To emphasise how unusual the so-called 'demonstration sponge' is,

the speaker describes it as being | | **15**

RESEARCH BEING CARRIED OUT ON SPONGES

Researchers are investigating what they call | | **16** | interaction.

Research into sponges may help people because

| | **17** | may be produced as a result.

Part 3

You will hear part of a radio programme in which guidebooks are discussed. For questions **18–22**, choose the answer (**A**, **B**, **C** or **D**) which fits best according to what you hear.

18   What recent development connected with travel is discussed initially?

    A   an increase in the types of adventurous holidays on offer
    B   destinations that have become cheaper
    C   improvements in what is offered in certain places
    D   a rise in the number of guidebooks

    18

19   John feels that the most important factor in choosing a guidebook is

    A   the reputation of the publisher.
    B   the attention to detail.
    C   the quality of the illustrations.
    D   the author's experience.

    19

20   What does John say he has discovered from comparing guidebooks?

    A   Some leave out interesting places altogether.
    B   Some use a strange style to describe places.
    C   Some fail to provide useful information.
    D   Some are not very enjoyable to read.

    20

21   What does the presenter say about the information in Blueprint Guides?

    A   It is sometimes hard to find what you need.
    B   Some of it is incomprehensible.
    C   Too much is in the form of ordinary narrative.
    D   The amount of detail can be excessive.

    21

22   John thinks that the style of writing in guidebooks should be

    A   both informal and authoritative.
    B   lively at all times.
    C   both objective and impersonal.
    D   undemanding of the reader.

    22

Part 4

You will hear two friends, Tim and Vera, discussing a concert which was held in the dark. For questions **23–28**, decide whether the opinions are expressed by only one of the speakers, or whether the speakers agree.

Write   **T**   for Tim,

           V   for Vera,

or   **B**   for Both, where they agree.

---

23   The lack of visual distractions allowed me to experience the music in a new way. | 23 |

24   I think I might listen to music in a different way from now on. | 24 |

25   The intimacy of the situation was unnerving. | 25 |

26   The performers must feel more relaxed knowing that they are not being observed. | 26 |

27   This experiment is not easily transferable to other media. | 27 |

28   'Dinners in the Dark' promises to be a less serious affair. | 28 |

PAPER 5   SPEAKING (19 minutes)

There are two examiners. One (the Interlocutor) conducts the test, providing you with the necessary materials and explaining what you have to do. The other examiner (the Assessor) will be introduced to you, but then takes no further part in the interaction.

Part 1 (3 minutes)

The Interlocutor first asks you and your partner a few questions which focus on information about yourselves and personal opinions.

Part 2 (4 minutes)

In this part of the test you and your partner are asked to talk together. The Interlocutor places a set of pictures on the table in front of you. This stimulus provides the basis for a discussion. The Interlocutor first asks an introductory question which focuses on one or two of the pictures. After about a minute, the Interlocutor gives you both a decision-making task based on the same set of pictures.

The pictures for Part 2 are on pages C4–C5 of the colour section.

Part 3 (12 minutes)

You are each given the opportunity to talk for two minutes, to comment after your partner has spoken and to take part in a more general discussion.

The Interlocutor gives you a card with a question written on it and asks you to talk about it for two minutes. After you have spoken, your partner is first asked to comment and then the Interlocutor asks you both another question related to the topic on the card. This procedure is repeated, so that your partner receives a card and speaks for two minutes, you are given an opportunity to comment and a follow-up question is asked.

Finally, the Interlocutor asks some further questions, which leads to a discussion on a general theme related to the subjects already covered in Part 3.

The cards for Part 3 are on pages C2 and C10 of the colour section.

Test 3

PAPER 1   READING (1 hour 30 minutes)

Part 1

For questions **1–18**, read the three texts below and decide which answer (**A, B, C** or **D**) best fits each gap.

Mark your answers **on the separate answer sheet**.

Art on TV

Why is it that television so consistently fails when it **(1)** …. to programmes about the visual arts? Painting and sculpture should be **(2)** …. subjects for the camera, which has the ability to show a whole work of art, then move in close to examine the details. Yet I can think of few series on television that have managed to **(3)** …. both the pleasure and complexity of looking at them.

A good example of what goes wrong can be seen in Robert Hughes's eight part survey of American art, *American Visions*. Hughes is a critic you can trust, he has a personality that commands attention and he has been given nearly eight hours in which to **(4)** …. British audiences to a school of art that British galleries have totally ignored. I had expected the series to **(5)** …. on great works of art. What I got instead was one about the way American history and culture are **(6)** …. in its art and architecture.

1 A applies	**B** takes	**C** addresses	**D** comes
2 A natural	**B** due	**C** right	**D** apparent
3 A convey	**B** inflict	**C** cast	**D** emit
4 A acquaint	**B** disclose	**C** reveal	**D** introduce
5 A target	**B** focus	**C** aim	**D** cover
6 A borne	**B** conferred	**C** reflected	**D** hinted

Dealing in Metals

For 20 years I worked as an international metals dealer and gained something of a reputation as a speculator. Metals are **(7)** …. far less than other markets. With a bit of luck, a **(8)** …. to take a risk and a good understanding of how the market works, it's possible to make a lot of money. Risk-taking is part and **(9)** …. of the industry. The buccaneering culture **(10)** …. nicely with a free-market global economy. But now the free-trade economists who claimed the market itself would maintain the price of scarce metals have found the opposite is happening. More minerals are being **(11)** …., and the cost of raw materials is decreasing. Taking inflation into account, the prices of most metals are about half of what they were 20 years ago. Recently, I was asked to look into **(12)** …. made against one of the multinational conglomerates that benefit from these cheap raw materials.

7 A ruled	**B** regulated	**C** governed	**D** legislated
8 A talent	**B** gift	**C** willingness	**D** propensity
9 A portion	**B** package	**C** present	**D** parcel
10 A plays	**B** joins	**C** fits	**D** suits
11 A expelled	**B** extracted	**C** exhumed	**D** expanded
12 A propositions	**B** allegations	**C** suggestions	**D** insinuations

Extract from a Holiday Brochure

Abaco and its off-shore cays are part of the 700 islands of the Bahamas that stretch from Florida, past the Tropic of Cancer, to Cuba. Each one has its own **(13)** …. , each one has something to offer.

The key to getting anywhere in the islands and cays of Abaco is a boat. If you don't get one **(14)** …. in with the room don't worry. Be happy. There are ferries **(15)** …. . And water-taxis. Or, there are plenty of boats to rent if you prefer to go under your own **(16)** …. .

But sailing is the most popular **(17)** …. of transport here. Abaco is nicknamed 'The Sailing Capital of the World' for good reason.

Those calm, naturally protected waters are also a paradise for fishing, diving, snorkelling and swimming. The cays and their beaches stretch for 200 miles like a **(18)** …. of pearls. It's not only at sea that gems can be found. At night it's the lights of the restaurants and cafés of Hope Town and Green Turtle Cay that sparkle.

13 A trait	**B** personality	**C** type	**D** distinction
14 A pushed	**B** given	**C** thrown	**D** bought
15 A sundry	**B** galore	**C** legion	**D** replete
16 A propulsion	**B** means	**C** momentum	**D** steam
17 A mode	**B** pattern	**C** way	**D** manner
18 A thread	**B** filament	**C** line	**D** string

Part 2

You are going to read four extracts which are all concerned in some way with people's attitudes. For questions **19–26**, choose the answer (**A**, **B**, **C** or **D**) which you think fits best according to the text.

Mark your answers **on the separate answer sheet**.

Food

There is something very elemental and satisfying about our relationship with food. I know I may be preaching to the converted, because presumably people keen on cooking buy cookery books like this one, but so often we imagine that, unless it is some special occasion or an especially elaborate dish, it is hardly worth attempting. Not so. Just by throwing a few roughly chopped carrots, a leek, some celery and a few herbs into water you will get the most delicious soup. This is much more satisfying than buying a packet or opening a tin. Instead of buying an over-sweet chocolate mousse full of preservatives, emulsifiers and additives, in five minutes you can turn out the most delicious confection that both grown-ups and children will love.

Cooking is also an offering, and it is a gesture of care and love to bring one's own creation, however humble or simple, to the table. Sharing food is so rich in symbolism, of our deepest human needs, that it is hardly surprising all our festivities and celebrations take place around tables, be they birthdays, anniversaries, engagements or whatever! No one would have a takeaway for a wedding or anniversary party! Nor would many people wish to have a business deal discussed over tinned soup.

19 What does the writer acknowledge about his readership?

    A They may already agree with him.
    B They may have varied attitudes to food.
    C They may have a preference for certain kinds of food.
    D They may be most interested in complicated meals.

20 The writer mentions tinned soup as an example of food which may

    A satisfy a number of people.
    B create the wrong impression.
    C be easy to prepare.
    D be economical to use.

In the Elevator

This morning, Alistair had made a stab at straightening up his office, but correspondence still littered every surface. Quarterly tax forms, state and federal, bulged out of desk drawers and cardboard boxes, all waiting on a day when he was in the filing mode. And then there was all the added paperwork that went along with owning an apartment building. The hundred-odd books and a few years' worth of journals were only in proximity to the new bookshelves.

As the elevator bore him closer to his floor, he knew that Mallory would be on time for their appointment. She would be knocking on the door of his empty office on the hour, not a second before or after. She was as compulsive about time as she was about neatness.

How would she react to the mess? She might assume he'd been vandalised. He could walk in behind her and feign shock.

Mrs Wilson, his cleaning woman, had arrived while he was scrambling around on the floor, trying desperately to clear a few square feet of the carpet. Putting his head out of the office door as she was turning her key in the lock of his apartment, he had smiled at her, his eyes filled with hope. Her own eyes had turned hard. Fat chance I'm going in there, said the back of her head as she had disappeared into his residence, which was her territory and all that she might be held accountable for.

He knew Mrs Wilson believed him to be a visitor from somewhere else, perhaps some point straight up, miles out, but nowhere on the surface of her own earth, which was square and shaped by the streets of Brooklyn.

21   One thing that occurred to Alistair about his office was that

    A   he had forgotten to put away some important documents there.
    B   he would have to do a lot of paperwork when he got back there.
    C   he had nowhere to put the books and journals.
    D   he could pretend to be surprised at its condition.

22   What had happened between Alistair and Mrs Wilson that morning?

    A   She had made it clear that she did not feel responsible for his office.
    B   She had told him that she was not willing to help him.
    C   She had not been as friendly to him as she usually was.
    D   She had decided that he was not like other people she knew.

KAREN

It was a simple desire – not to be like her mother – that led Karen to create her own story, her own mythology, a mythology of difference and strength. In the tale that she constructed for herself, there were significant moments in her progress; such as the day she was twelve years old and her brother quick-swung a golf club behind him and hit her full in the eye. At the first moment of impact, she was convinced of immediate blindness. But the bone had protected her, as the doctor from the high-walled house later assured her. The golf club had clean missed the eye and she was left with only a few stitches that healed to a pale drawing of past suffering. When she opened her eyes in the doctor's white-walled consulting room, overlooking the tennis courts, and saw her mother clear before her, muttering predictably and paradoxically about both miracles and small mercies, she knew that she was saved for some purpose.

23 What was characteristic of Karen's 'mythology'?

    A   the portrayal of herself as a victim
    B   the models she chose for herself
    C   the importance attached to particular events
    D   the carelessness of the people around her

24 In the doctor's consulting room, Karen's mother's behaviour

    A   was an embarrassment to Karen.
    B   came as no surprise to Karen.
    C   took Karen's mind off her situation.
    D   was a logical reaction to Karen's accident.

Visual materials for Paper 5

TEST 1

What makes people laugh?

- cultural background
- visual or verbal
- changing attitudes

TEST 2

How easy is it to remember new information?

- topic
- circumstances
- quantity

TEST 3

What it is that makes people powerful?

- personal circumstances
- knowledge
- personality

TEST 4

Why should dangerous sports be allowed?

- personal choice
- safety
- money

TEST 1 PAPER 5   **Teenage magazine – People and animals**

2A

2B

2C

© Andy Drysdale/REX FEATURES

2A

2B

2C

3A

3B

3C

3D

© RESO/REX FEATURES

3E

3F

4A

4B

4C

4D

4E

4F

TEST 1

How important is it to have a sense of humour?

- health
- time and place
- relationships

TEST 2

What makes a place particularly memorable?

- personal experiences
- people
- atmosphere

TEST 3

How much do people respect authority nowadays?

- different societies
- changing times
- influences

TEST 4

What helps people to deal with difficult situations?

- personality
- support
- age

TEST 4

Prompt card 4c

In what ways has life become more or less dangerous?

- technology
- health
- social values

Miss Fogerty

Miss Fogerty, returning briskly to her duties across the wet grass of the village green, was both excited and saddened by the scene she had just witnessed. It is always exhilarating to be the first to know something of note, particularly in a small community, and Miss Fogerty's quiet life held little excitement. On the other hand, her grief for Dr Bailey's condition was overwhelming. He had attended her for many years and she remembered with gratitude his concern for her annual bouts of laryngitis which were, fortunately, about the only troubles for which she had to consult him.

His most valuable quality, Miss Fogerty considered, was his making one feel that there was always plenty of time, and that he truly wished to hear about his patients' fears and perplexities. It was this quality, above all others, which had so endeared the good doctor to the village and its environs. He had always been prepared to give – of his time, of his knowledge, and of his humour. His reward had been outstanding loyalty and affection.

25   As Miss Fogerty crossed the grass, her predominant feeling was one of

    A   confusion.
    B   sorrow.
    C   excitement.
    D   relief.

26   Miss Fogerty felt that Dr Bailey was particularly liked for his

    A   loyalty to his patients.
    B   ability to say the right things.
    C   independence of thought.
    D   generosity of spirit.

Part 3

You are going to read an extract from a novel. Seven paragraphs have been removed from the extract. Choose from the paragraphs **A–H** the one which fits each gap (**27–33**). There is one extra paragraph which you do not need to use.

Mark your answers **on the separate answer sheet**.

THE WELL

I had read somewhere that from a sufficiently deep hole, one could see the stars, if the day were clear. I had persuaded you to help me with my scheme; you watched, eyes wide, fist to mouth, as I winched up the well bucket, steadied it on the wall and then climbed in. I told you to let me down. I had not thought to allow for the bucket's much increased weight, your lack of strength or inclination to just stand back and let what would happen, happen. You held the handle, taking some of the strain as I pushed the bucket off the side of the well's stone surround. Freed of the wall's support, I plunged immediately. You gave a little shriek and made one attempt to brake the handle, then you let it go. I fell into the well. I cracked my head.

27	

At the time I was at first just dazed, then frightened, then relieved, then finally both angry at you for letting me fall and afraid of what Mother would say. You called down, asking if I was all right. I opened my mouth to shout, and then you called again, a note of rising panic in your voice, and with those words stopped mine in my throat. I lay still, eyelids cracked enough to watch you through the foliage of lashes. You disappeared, calling out for help. I waited a moment, then quickly hauled and pushed my way to the top, then pulled myself over the edge and landed on the courtyard cobbles.

28	

Mother and Father both appeared along with you and old Arthur; Mother shrieked, flapping her hands. Father shouted and told Arthur to haul on the winch handle. You stood back, looking pale and shocked, watching. I was bowed in the shadows. A fire of fierce elation filled me. Then I saw the line of drops I'd left, from the well to where I now stood. I looked in horror

at the spots, dark coins of dirty well water fallen from my soaking clothes on to the dry, grey cobbles. At my feet, in the darkness, the water had formed a little pool.

29	

This had quickly become more serious than I'd anticipated, escalating with dizzying rapidity from a great prank born of a brilliant brainwave to something that would not be put to rest without some serious, painful and lasting punishment being inflicted on somebody, almost certainly myself. I cursed myself for not thinking this through. From crafty plan, to downfall, to wheeze, to calamity; all in a few minutes.

30	

Sitting up, comforted, my head in my weeping mother's bosom, I went 'Phew' and said 'Oh dear' and smiled bravely and claimed that I had found a secret tunnel from the bottom of the well to the moat, and crawled and swum along it until I got out, climbed up the bridge and tottered, exhausted, through the passageway.

31	

Thinking I was plugging a gap, in fact only adding another log to my pyre, I said that the secret passage had fallen in after me; there wouldn't be any point in, say, sending somebody down to look for it. In fact the whole well was dangerous. I'd barely escaped with my life. I looked into my father's eyes and it was like looking into a dark tunnel with no stars at the end.

32	

My words died in my throat. 'Don't be ridiculous, boy,' he said, investing more contempt in those few words than I'd have thought a whole language capable of conveying. He rose smoothly to his feet and walked away.

33	

In that pity was a rebuke as severe and wounding as that my father had administered, and in as much that it confirmed that this was the mature judgement of my actions and my father's, not some aberration I might be able to discount or ignore, it affected me even more profoundly.

A I looked back into the courtyard, to where Father was now shining a flashlight down into the well and peering into the gloom. The drops I had left shone in the sunlight. I could not believe that nobody had seen them. Mother was screaming hysterically now; a sharp, jarring noise that I had never heard before. It shook my soul, suffused my conscience. What was I to do? I had had my revenge on you, but where did I go from here?

B To this day I think I was almost getting away with it until Father appeared squatting in front of me. He had me repeat my story. I did so, hesitating. His eyes narrowed.

C It did not occur to me then that I had succeeded, in a sense, in my plan. What I saw were lights, strange, inchoate and bizarre. It was only later that I connected the visual symptoms of that fall and impact with the stylised stars and planets I was used to seeing drawn in a cartoon panel whenever a comic character suffered a similar whack.

D It was as though he was seeing me for the first time, and as though I was looking down a secret passage through time, to an adult perspective, to the way the world and cocky, lying children's stories would look to me when I was his age.

E That was what racked me, spread upon the castle's stones; that was what gripped me like a cold fist inside and squeezed those cold and bitter tears of grief from me and could not be comforted by Mother's soothing strokes and gentle pats and soft cooings.

F The plan came to me like a lifebelt to a drowning man. I gathered all my courage and left my hiding place, coming staggering out and blinking. I cried out faintly, one hand to my brow, then yelled out a little louder when my first cry went unheeded. I stumbled on a little further, then collapsed dramatically on the cobbles.

G I could hear raised, alarmed voices coming from the castle's main door. I ran the opposite way, down to the passage leading to the moat bridge, and hid in the shadows there.

H Arthur looked down at me, his expression regretful and troubled, shaking his head or looking like he wanted to, not because I had had a terrifying adventure and then been unjustly disbelieved by my own father, but because he too could see through my forlorn and hapless lie, and worried for the soul, the character, the future moral standing of any child so shameless – and so incompetent – in its too easily resorted-to lying.

Part 4

You are going to read an extract from a book on art. For questions **34–40**, choose the answer (**A**, **B**, **C** or **D**) which you think fits best according to the text.

Mark your answers **on the separate answer sheet**.

AESTHETICS

line 1 By one of the ironic perversities that often attend the course of affairs, the existence of the works of art upon which formation of aesthetic theory depends has become an obstruction to theory about them. For one reason: these works are products that exist externally and physically. In common conception, the work of art is often identified with the building, book, painting, or statue in its existence apart from human experience. Since the actual work of art is what the product does with and in experience, the result is not favourable to understanding. In addition, the very perfection of some of these products, the prestige they possess because of a long history of unquestioned admiration, creates conventions that get in the way of fresh insight. When an art product once attains classic status, it somehow becomes isolated from the human conditions under which it was brought into being and from the human consequences it engenders in actual life experience.

When artistic objects are separated from both conditions of origin and operation in experience, a wall is built around them that renders almost opaque their general significance, with which aesthetic theory deals. Art is remitted to a separate realm, where it is cut off from that association with the materials and aims of every other form of human effort and achievement.

line 27 A primary task is thus imposed upon one who undertakes to write upon the philosophy of the fine arts. This task is to restore continuity between the refined and intensified forms of experience that are works of art and the everyday events, doings, and sufferings that are universally recognised to constitute experience. Mountain peaks do not float unsupported; they do not even just rest upon the earth. They *are* the earth in one of its manifest operations. It is the business of those who are concerned with the theory of the earth, geographers and geologists, to make this fact evident in its various implications. The theorist who would deal philosophically with fine art has a like task to accomplish.

If one is willing to grant this position, even if only by way of temporary experiment, one will see that there follows a conclusion which is at first sight surprising. In order to understand the meaning of artistic products, we have to forget them for a time, to turn aside from them and have recourse to the ordinary forces and conditions of experience that we do not usually regard as aesthetic. We must arrive at the theory of art by means of a detour. For theory is concerned with understanding and insight. It is, of course, quite possible to enjoy flowers in their coloured form and delicate fragrance without knowing anything about plants theoretically. But if one sets out to *understand* the flowering of plants, one is committed to finding out something about the interactions of soil, air, water and sunlight that condition the growth of plants.

In order to *understand* the aesthetic in its ultimate and approved forms, one must begin with it in the raw; in the events and scenes that hold the attentive eye and ear, arousing one's interest and affording enjoyment as one looks and listens. Yet so extensive and subtly pervasive are the ideas that set art itself upon a remote pedestal that many people would be repelled rather than pleased if told that they enjoyed their casual recreations, in part at least, because of their aesthetic quality. The arts which today have most vitality for the average person are things he or she does not take to be arts: for instance, the movies, jazz, comic strips, and, too frequently, lurid newspaper accounts of the week's events. For, when what they know as art is relegated to the museum and gallery, the unconquerable impulse towards experiences enjoyable in themselves finds such outlet as the daily environment provides. Many people who protest against the museum conception of art still share the fallacy from which that conception springs. For the popular notion comes from a separation of art from the objects and scenes of ordinary experience that many theorists and critics pride themselves upon holding and even elaborating. The times when select and distinguished objects are closely connected with the products of usual vocations are the times when appreciation of the former is most rife and most keen.

34 What 'ironic perversity' is referred to in line 1?

    A The formation of aesthetic theory depends on the existence of works of art.
    B The very existence of works of art interferes with thinking about them.
    C Too wide a range of objects are considered to be works of art.
    D Works of art have a tendency to generate misunderstandings.

35 According to the writer, what happens when an art product attains classic status?

    A The difficulties involved in its creation are underestimated.
    B The prestige it enjoys begins to attract criticism.
    C It loses its connection with common experience.
    D It ceases to have a provocative effect on observers.

36 What is the 'primary task' referred to in line 27?

    A making sure that art does not surrender its role in society
    B encouraging ordinary people to realise the significance of art
    C shedding light on the aesthetic aims of artists
    D explaining the link between art and ordinary life

37 The writer mentions mountain peaks to demonstrate that

    A works of art do not exist in isolation.
    B writers on art face a difficult challenge.
    C art has much in common with other disciplines.
    D theorists have a responsibility to be accurate.

38 Why is the conclusion about understanding artistic products in paragraph 3 described as surprising?

    A It ignores certain types of art products.
    B It involves the use of unexpected criteria.
    C It undervalues the emotional response to art.
    D It conflicts with the opinions of theorists on fine art.

39 What does the writer intend us to learn from the reference to flowers?

    A Art can be enjoyed without being explained.
    B Only committed individuals can learn to appreciate art.
    C True works of art are only created in suitable conditions.
    D Failure to enjoy art makes a theoretical understanding difficult.

40 According to the writer, setting art on a remote pedestal has meant that

    A people enjoy works of art less than they would otherwise do.
    B casual recreations are preferred to the study of art.
    C aesthetic qualities in other areas of life go unnoticed.
    D people are happy to consign art to museums and galleries.

PAPER 2   WRITING (2 hours)

Part 1

You **must** answer this question. Write your answer in **300–350** words in an appropriate style.

---

1 You have read the extract below as part of a newspaper article on education. Readers have been asked to send in their opinions. You decide to write a letter responding to the points raised and expressing your own views.

> Some people consider that much of our school education is a waste of time. These people argue that we are only motivated to learn what is relevant and useful to us based on our experience. Therefore, as most of our education happens at such an early age, it is surely necessary to rethink what people *really* need to learn at school.

Write your **letter**. Do not write any postal addresses.

Part 2

Write an answer to **one** of the questions **2–5** in this part. Write your answer in **300–350** words in an appropriate style.

---

2 In order to celebrate the history and culture of your city, the council has decided to commemorate the achievements of a person, well known locally, who was born, or worked in the area. It has invited the public to send in proposals stating who they think should be chosen and in what ways his or her life should be celebrated.

Write your **proposal**.

3 You have recently visited a museum or exhibition, either in your country or abroad. Write a review for an English language magazine, describing the contents of the museum or exhibition. You should say whether it is worth visiting and explain why museums or exhibitions are an important part of national culture.

Write your **review**.

4 A popular magazine is asking people to submit articles on their favourite leisure activities. You decide to send an article on your favourite leisure pursuit, which you hope will interest and entertain other readers, as well as encourage them to take up the activity themselves.

Write your **article**.

5 Based on your reading of **one** of these books, write on **one** of the following:

(a)   Anne Tyler: *The Accidental Tourist*
As part of your studies your tutor has asked you to write an essay on the way Alexander is being brought up by Muriel and to come to some conclusions about what has particularly influenced the development of his personality.

Write your **essay**.

(b)   L.P. Hartley: *The Go-Between*
You belong to a reading group whose members have decided to study novels which portray English society in different historical periods. You decide to suggest *The Go-Between* as a suitable text and to write a report for the group in which you describe how social attitudes and conventions at the time of Leo's childhood are illustrated in the novel.

Write your **report**.

(c)   Brian Moore: *The Colour of Blood*
An arts magazine is planning a series of articles on great heroes in modern literature. You feel that Cardinal Bem displays qualities that make him a hero and decide to write an article in support of your view.

Write your **article**.

PAPER 3   USE OF ENGLISH (1 hour 30 minutes)

Part 1

For questions **1–15**, read the text below and think of the word which best fits each space. Use only **one** word in each space. There is an example at the beginning **(0)**.

Write your answers in CAPITAL LETTERS **on the separate answer sheet**.

Example: | **0** | A | S | | | | | | | | | | | | | | | | |

Communication

Throughout our lives, right from the moment when **(0)**.....*as*..... infants we cry to express hunger, we are engaging in social interaction of one form or **(1)**............ . Each and **(2)**............ time we encounter fellow human beings, some kind of social interaction will take place, **(3)**............ it's getting on a bus and paying the fare for the journey, or socialising with friends. It goes without **(4)**............ , therefore, that we need the ability to communicate. Without some method of transmitting intentions, we would be **(5)**............ a complete loss when it **(6)**............ to interacting socially.

Communication involves the exchange of information, which can be **(7)**............ from a gesture to a friend signalling boredom to the presentation of a university thesis which may **(8)**............ ever be read by a handful of others, or it could be something in **(9)**............ the two.

Our highly developed languages set us **(10)**............ from animals. **(11)**............ for these languages, we could not communicate sophisticated or abstract ideas. **(12)**............ could we talk or write about people or objects **(13)**............ immediately present. **(14)**............ we restricted to discussing objects already present, we would be **(15)**............ to make abstract generalisations about the world.

Part 2

For questions **16–25**, read the text below. Use the word given in capitals at the end of some of the lines to form a word that fits in the space in the same line. There is an example at the beginning **(0)**.

Write your answers in CAPITAL LETTERS **on the separate answer sheet**.

Example: | 0 | C | O | M | P | A | R | A | T | I | V | E | L | Y | | | | | | |

Science and technology

Until **(0)**.....*comparatively*..... recent times science and technology performed **COMPARE**
different and separate functions, the progress of one so often completely
(16)............ to the progress of the other. **RELATE**

(17)............ have established that, since the earliest times, the improvements **HISTORY**
in our way of life have resulted from an empirical approach, that is a process of
trial and error, by which equipment and tools are made to satisfy important
needs. It is to this approach that we owe the evolution of technology. Our modern
concept of science, both **(18)**............ and pragmatic in approach, stems from **PHILOSOPHY**
the seventeenth century, when extensive investigations into the natural laws
governing the behaviour of matter were **(19)**............ . **TAKE**

It was this **(20)**............ style of thought which led to a science-based technology. **REVOLUTION**
Scientific knowledge was not in itself seen as a **(21)**............ for the earlier system **PLACE**
of trial and error, but it did help the technical **(22)**............ to see which path of **INNOVATE**
experimentation might be more **(23)**............ . With the industrialisation of the **FRUIT**
nineteenth century, the bond between science and technology **(24)**............ . **STRONG**
In our own time, the mutual **(25)**............ of one discipline upon the other has **RELY**
increased still further.

Part 3

For questions **26–31**, think of **one** word only which can be used appropriately in all three sentences. Here is an example **(0)**.

Example:

0 Some of the tourists are hoping to get compensation for the poor state of the hotel, and I think they have a very .... case.

There's no point in trying to wade across the river, the current is far too ....

If you're asking me which of the candidates should get the job, I'm afraid I don't have any .... views either way.

0	S	T	R	O	N	G												

Write **only** the missing word in CAPITAL LETTERS **on the separate answer sheet**.

---

26 You can always .... on family members to help you out.

It is always important to .... your change before you leave the shop.

I .... you as one of my closest friends.

27 The actress forgot her .... on the opening night of the play.

This anti-ageing cream will reduce .... on your face.

Don't ever cross railway .... at this point; it's far too dangerous.

28 When David heard the news, he was in a terrible .... until his wife managed to calm him down.

Each prospective member .... has to accept certain obligations in order to join the confederation.

The plans for the renovation of the house really depend on the .... of the foundations.

29   I have the ……………………… that some members of the group are less than happy with the planned excursion.

Vaclav did his best to leave the conference audience with a positive ……………………… of the work of his organisation.

On one of the Roman tiles you can see the ……………………… of a dog's paw, made before the clay had dried over two thousand years ago.

30   Whether the book in ……………………… is the one published in the USA is something you'll have to find out from the librarian.

There's no ……………………… of Thea's loyalty to the company; she has been with them for the past 15 years, after all.

It took the minister some time to finally address the ……………………… of underfunding in education.

31   Liam won't be playing for the team this week – he ……………………… a muscle in last week's match.

Christl was angry because she ……………………… her dress on the door handle when she was getting into the car.

Paco ……………………… out of the house this morning – he must have got up late again.

Part 4

For questions **32–39**, complete the second sentence so that it has a similar meaning to the first sentence, using the word given. **Do not change the word given.** You must use between **three** and **eight** words, including the word given.

Here is an example **(0)**.

Example:

0 Do you mind if I watch you while you paint?

objection

Do you .... you while you paint?

0	*have any objection to my watching*

Write **only** the missing words **on the separate answer sheet**.

---

32   Nobody wants to buy second-hand computer equipment these days.

call

There is .... second-hand computer equipment these days.

33   This letter clearly says that you are entitled to attend the meeting.

right

This letter makes .... attend the meeting.

34   Martina was very annoyed that her son had borrowed her new bike.

great

To .... borrowed her new bike.

35 You should never leave this door unlocked under any circumstances.

is

Under ………………………………………………………………… left unlocked.

36 There is every certainty that Joel will have finished the report by Monday.

bound

Joel …………………………………………………………… by Monday.

37 One day she's going to become a famous film star.

matter

It's only …………………………………………………………… a famous film star.

38 Because of the appalling weather conditions, some trains will be delayed.

subject

Some trains ……………………………………………………………… because of the appalling weather conditions.

39 I don't mind which make of car you choose.

consequence

It …………………………………………………………………… make of car you choose.

Part 5

For questions **40–44**, read the following texts on television. For questions **40–43**, answer with a word or short phrase. You do not need to write complete sentences. For question **44**, write a summary according to the instructions given.

Write your answers to questions **40–44 on the separate answer sheet**.

Supporters of television have always promoted it as a tool of public edification, an inexpensive provider of the best in drama, music and, of course, the news. In reality, however, it falls somewhat short of such ideals. Flipping through my eight channels late one sleepless night, I didn't find the best of anything, quite the opposite in fact.   line 5

There is good television out there, though. Much of what we see is pleasant and relaxing – or at least harmless. And there is even a little bit of great television, which can make us rethink important social and political issues, or make us laugh until we forget about them. And even if the majority of what's on television is mundane, what it says about the viewing public is not. When television condones or censors, it is measuring the opinion of at least part of the population; when audiences boycott certain shows, they are demonstrating the other side of television's interactivity. And when the entire nation gets caught up in   line 14
the life of a soap character who isn't even a real person, it's more than a meaningless fad; we care about our TV because we identify so closely with it. We should recognise but understand its failures, as we do our own.

40   In your own words, explain what the writer is referring to when he says 'quite the opposite in fact'. (line 5)

....

41   In your own words, explain what the writer means by 'television's interactivity'. (line 14)

....

If we can't be celebrities ourselves, we at least like to think we know one. 'He's a really nice person,' we say, with great authority, divulging some little detail to confirm our familiarity. Such information is what the TV programme *Through the Keyhole* provides.

Whispering in confidential insinuations, the presenter takes us through a celebrity's house in their absence, casting spotlights on their lifestyle and personality that reveal their taste, or lack of it. His manner alternates between admiration and sneering superiority. The person is then unveiled to a studio audience and joins in the discussion. All of this is intended to let the viewers feel they are on intimate terms with the celebrity and privy to all kinds of personal details. First you see their music collection, bookshelves and curtains, and then hear convivial conversation.

This, of course, is not the first show in which we've been invited to fraternise with the famous in their own habitats. Indeed, the proliferation of such series would tend to confirm that TV has found a way of yet further extending that central role it has come to play in our social relations. Having created the celebrities in the first place, it now allows us to spend time in their company; these surrogate acquaintances taking the place of the real people we might just meet if we had the courage to hit the switch and venture forth into society. Sometimes we marvel at the opulence of their existence, more often we are reassured to find they are just ordinary people, much like us in fact. But most of all, we are able to say, 'They are really nice people.'

42   In your own words, explain why the presenter of *Through the Keyhole* might sometimes feel 'superiority' (line 8) towards the celebrities featured in the programme.

....

43   Which two phrases in the second paragraph reinforce the idea of 'familiarity' (line 3) with the celebrities?

....

44   In a paragraph of **50–70** words, summarise **in your own words as far as possible** the ways in which, according to **both** texts, television plays a role in contemporary society, beyond that of entertaining people. Write your summary **on the separate answer sheet**.

PAPER 4 LISTENING (40 minutes approximately)

Part 1

You will hear four different extracts. For questions **1–8**, choose the answer (**A**, **B** or **C**) which fits best according to what you hear. There are two questions for each extract.

Extract One

You hear part of a talk about employment opportunities for actors.

1 The speaker says that most actors who take temporary jobs do so because they

    A have to satisfy financial needs.
    B want to broaden their experience.
    C feel unsure about their commitment to acting.

    `1`

2 He says the most satisfactory temporary jobs

    A are found by actors' agents.
    B help raise actors' profiles.
    C exploit actors' existing skills.

    `2`

Extract Two

You hear someone being interviewed about what's called 'muzak', the type of recorded background music often heard in public places.

3 According to Richard Atwell, how does 'new art muzak' compare to ordinary muzak?

    A It is less intrusive.
    B It is equally accessible.
    C It is more carefully chosen.

    `3`

4 What do the two speakers disagree about?

    A the role of muzak in shops
    B the importance of silence in restaurants
    C the need to improve people's working environment

    `4`

Extract Three

You hear part of a talk about improving concentration.

5 The speaker's advice focuses on

   A a sequence of tasks.
   B a method of relaxing.
   C a change of routine.

| | 5 |

6 According to the speaker, concentration is particularly affected by

   A visual stimuli.
   B emotion.
   C silence.

| | 6 |

Extract Four

You hear part of a radio programme about the theatre.

7 Who is being interviewed?

   A an actor
   B a playwright
   C a director

| | 7 |

8 What is the man doing when he speaks?

   A accepting a criticism
   B denying an accusation
   C defending a point of view

| | 8 |

Part 2

You will hear part of a radio programme about a wildlife conservation project located in a disused industrial port. For questions **9–17**, complete the sentences with a word or short phrase.

Previous industries in Harford included the processing of both oil and

	9

Tony says that the port complex closed largely because

| | **10** | were getting smaller.

The Marine Wildlife Trust was set up to raise awareness of the

| | **11** | of the sea.

At first, the port owners worried about the

| | **12** | implications of accommodating the seals.

The Marine Wildlife Trust persuaded the port owners that accepting the seals would be

beneficial for their | | **13** |

The viruses affecting the seals are often spread by

| | **14** | which have fallen into the sea.

Tony says that the seals recover because they are provided with a

| | **15** | and good food.

Tony feels that the requirements for his job are a suitable background, a lot of

| | **16** | and a knowledge of toxins.

Tony describes the seals in the complex as less

| | **17** | than people expect.

Part 3

You will hear part of an interview in which a professor of sociology is talking about the subject of leisure in Britain. For questions **18–22**, choose the answer (**A**, **B**, **C** or **D**) which fits best according to what you hear.

---

18   According to Professor Marshall, leisure is increasingly being seen as a way of

    A   convincing people they have freedom of choice.
    B   helping people to understand themselves better.
    C   encouraging people to perform better at work.
    D   dissuading people from challenging authority.

	18

19   According to US sociologists, 'serious leisure' is an activity which

    A   is detrimental to someone's work.
    B   becomes a financial burden.
    C   becomes the central focus of someone's life.
    D   helps a person to achieve a higher income.

	19

20   Professor Marshall believes that as people become more involved in their chosen leisure activities,

    A   they are less afraid of the dangers.
    B   they place a greater value on routine.
    C   they worry less about the rules.
    D   they want more scope for personal development.

	20

21   According to Professor Marshall, television

    A   provides a useful basis for social interaction.
    B   can disrupt other leisure activities.
    C   is no more than a very passive activity.
    D   destroys meaningful conversation.

	21

22   Professor Marshall says that having to wear special clothes to take part in a leisure activity may

    A   improve the participants' respect for each other.
    B   redefine the participants' social roles.
    C   increase the participants' self-esteem.
    D   reflect the priorities of the participants' work environment.

	22

Part 4

You will hear part of a radio programme in which two writers discuss the appeal of the short story. For questions **23–28**, decide whether the opinions are expressed by only one of the speakers, or whether the speakers agree.

Write   **C**   for Claire,
              A   for Alan,
or   **B**   for Both, where they agree.

23   I enjoy short stories because I like variety and quality. | | **23** |

24   Critics have often been inaccurate in their description of my style of writing. | | **24** |

25   The appeal of writing short stories is being able to explore the world from different standpoints. | | **25** |

26   Short story writing and poetry writing share some common features. | | **26** |

27   The skill involved in writing a novel is to develop the story lines. | | **27** |

28   The short story holds a particular appeal for some readers. | | **28** |

PAPER 5   SPEAKING (19 minutes)

There are two examiners. One (the Interlocutor) conducts the test, providing you with the necessary materials and explaining what you have to do. The other examiner (the Assessor) will be introduced to you, but then takes no further part in the interaction.

Part 1 (3 minutes)

The Interlocutor first asks you and your partner a few questions which focus on information about yourselves and personal opinions.

Part 2 (4 minutes)

In this part of the test you and your partner are asked to talk together. The Interlocutor places a set of pictures on the table in front of you. This stimulus provides the basis for a discussion. The Interlocutor first asks an introductory question which focuses on one or two of the pictures. After about a minute, the Interlocutor gives you both a decision-making task based on the same set of pictures.

The pictures for Part 2 are on pages C6–C7 of the colour section.

Part 3 (12 minutes)

You are each given the opportunity to talk for two minutes, to comment after your partner has spoken and to take part in a more general discussion.

The Interlocutor gives you a card with a question written on it and asks you to talk about it for two minutes. After you have spoken, your partner is first asked to comment and then the Interlocutor asks you both another question related to the topic on the card. This procedure is repeated, so that your partner receives a card and speaks for two minutes, you are given an opportunity to comment and a follow-up question is asked.

Finally, the Interlocutor asks some further questions, which leads to a discussion on a general theme related to the subjects already covered in Part 3.

The cards for Part 3 are on pages C2 and C10 of the colour section.

Test 4

PAPER 1   READING (1 hour 30 minutes)

Part 1

For questions **1–18**, read the three texts below and decide which answer (**A**, **B**, **C** or **D**) best fits each gap.

Mark your answers **on the separate answer sheet**.

Goat Racing

I was about to witness goat racing. Easter Monday in Buccoo Village. I was fighting my way through ice-cream vans, **(1)** …. of people, food stalls and hot music singeing my eardrums. Even though the general movement was towards the racecourse, I **(2)** …. my way through the crowds in an effort to get a good pitch. An area had been **(3)** …. to make a course for competitors. Not quite on a **(4)** …. with established racecourses, but on the similar assumption that spectators were to line either side of a **(5)** …. of ground along which the participants would travel. An attempt was being made to keep a handful of select goats in order. No mean feat when dealing with an animal fabled to eat almost anything it can get **(6)** …. of.

1 A flocks	**B** shoals	**C** hordes	**D** herds
2 A handed	**B** thumbed	**C** fingered	**D** elbowed
3 A cordoned off	**B** shut away	**C** penned in	**D** closed down
4 A standard	**B** rule	**C** par	**D** norm
5 A spread	**B** stretch	**C** space	**D** span
6 A grip	**B** hold	**C** hang	**D** grasp

Canoe Trip

As the day **(7)** …. to a close, I started to think about the night ahead, and I **(8)** …. with fear. The canoe was too wet to sleep in, there was nowhere to stop, and we hadn't seen any villages or huts since early morning. In the dim moonlight, and with the **(9)** …. of our torch we could just make out the line of the cliffs; the torch batteries were **(10)** …. , so we put in new ones, but they didn't work. Obviously we weren't going to be able to spot a camping place. A couple of miles later, Lesley called out that she had seen a distant flickering light and our hopes **(11)** …. : the light turned out to be moonlight glinting on waves; soon we could hear the roaring noise of fast-rushing water, though we couldn't see what was happening. Time **(12)** …. still, and we moved on.

7 A led	**B** pulled	**C** drew	**D** headed
8 A thumped	**B** beat	**C** throbbed	**D** shuddered
9 A support	**B** means	**C** backing	**D** aid
10 A dimming	**B** failing	**C** sinking	**D** fainting
11 A soared	**B** expanded	**C** reared	**D** ascended
12 A kept	**B** waited	**C** stood	**D** remained

How to be Presentation Perfect – we answer your questions

I am not a natural at making presentations, yet in my role as managing director I am increasingly required to present internally to my colleagues, (13) …. externally to the major shareholders. How can I improve my presentational techniques and my confidence?

You are not the only one. Making a presentation involves completely different skills from those you need to run a company, yet more and more senior executives are **(14)** …. to be accomplished at it.

If you are trying to convince your audience of something, you have to be convinced yourself. Demonstrate your conviction in the passion and enthusiasm you **(15)** …. to the presentation. That means you must do your homework. Test your proposition carefully in advance. Ask colleagues to identify the 'hard questions' your audience might **(16)** …. to you. You also need to build a positive climate from the **(17)** …. . Begin with an area of **(18)** …. ground that people can identify with and build gradually towards the conclusion you want to reach.

13 A let alone	**B** not to mention	**C** besides	**D** alongside
14 A demanded	**B** called	**C** expected	**D** desired
15 A bring	**B** bear	**C** convey	**D** deliver
16 A make	**B** request	**C** propose	**D** put
17 A outset	**B** outcome	**C** outlook	**D** output
18 A mutual	**B** common	**C** shared	**D** similar

Part 2

You are going to read four extracts which are all concerned in some way with the cinema. For questions **19–26**, choose the answer (**A**, **B**, **C** or **D**) which you think fits best according to the text.

Mark your answers **on the separate answer sheet**.

Every Picture Tells a Story

Adapting novels for film almost always involves a process of reduction, condensation and deletion. This can be very frustrating for the writer, but also illuminating. Working on a script, I was struck by how much of the dialogue and narrative description in a given scene in the novel I could dispense with, while still getting across the same point. This does not necessarily mean that the dialogue and description of the original were superfluous. It is a matter of the type of attention demanded of the audience by narrative in each medium, and a matter of the type of redundancy each employs. I do not mean 'redundancy' in the usual colloquial sense of material which is unnecessary, but in a technical sense.

In a novel, such redundancy would include the repeated allusion to certain traits by which characters are identified, as well as speech tags such as 'he said'. Strictly speaking a character trait needs to be described only once, but it assists comprehension if we are constantly reminded of it. And usually we can infer who is speaking in a scene of dialogue from the content and layout on the page, but speech tags make reading easier.

Stage drama, which consists mostly of speech, imitates and reproduces the redundancy of real speech with various degrees of stylisation. In some modern dramas, this is taken to an extreme, so that the dialogue seems to consist almost entirely of redundant language, whose function is purely phatic (merely establishing contact between the two speakers), leaving us in the dark as to what is being communicated.

19 The writer's experience of adaptation has shown him

    A   how tiresome changing mediums can be for a writer.
    B   how an audience can influence decisions about redundancy.
    C   that as a writer he depends too greatly on dialogue.
    D   that the nature of redundancy varies with the medium.

20 What approach do some playwrights take towards conversational redundancy?

    A   They ignore it.
    B   They exploit it.
    C   They use it inconsistently.
    D   They see it as a necessary tool.

Watching Movies

Watching movies, one can be carried away to the degree that one feels part of the world of the moving picture. It is an experience that lifts one out of oneself into a world where one is not beholden to ordinary reality, at least for the length of the film. So it seems that what one feels and does while at the movies does not really count.

But as soon as the lights are turned on, the spell is abruptly broken, one is again in the ordinary world. One does not feel responsible for the time spent under the spell of the film and, further, this unreality prevents one from devoting much serious attention to what was considered in my boyhood not an art, but 'mere entertainment'. This was how some people of our parents' generation, and most of our teachers, disparaged the movies. Like most people, they liked to be entertained, but they did not consider the movies to be an art.

21 The writer suggests that for the duration of a film

   A a unique set of circumstances prevails.
   B people feel able to behave irresponsibly.
   C people feel better able to cope with reality.
   D everyday events take on a new meaning.

22 What does the writer suggest about the perception of watching movies as 'mere entertainment' rather than art?

   A It was a short-sighted view without foundation.
   B It stemmed from the nature of the activity.
   C It was expressed by those who did not like the movies.
   D It reflected the quality of movies being shown.

The film studios

The site of the Leiper Film Company studios was a huddle of many disparate buildings. The topography of the place was irrational and obscure. It possessed, certainly, a few permanent landmarks such as the Script Department, but for the rest it appeared to be made up of numerous small rooms, identically furnished, which were employed for official and unofficial confabulations and could be distinguished one from another only by a surrealist system of digits and letters of the alphabet; and to locate any particular one of these unaided was a considerable enterprise. More than anything else, perhaps, the studio lacked a focus. A decisive single main entrance might have provided this, but in fact there were three main entrances, severely egalitarian in their amenities and with nothing to choose between them except that one of them gave access to the place where you wanted to arrive and the other two did not; and in none of them was there anywhere where enquiries could be made and some species of orientation established. To the mere stranger it was all vastly confusing.

Mere strangers, however, were few and far between; for obvious reasons, the organisation did not encourage their presence. And it was to be presumed that people who worked there could find their way about all right. And by these employees' united labours, romance and adventure would travel the country. Hand in hand, head against shoulder, Jane and George, Sally and Dick would, for three hours at least, snatch immunity, by the studio's contriving, from domestic contention and public strife, from tedium and malice and routine, and the struggle to keep alive.

23 Finding one's way around the studios

   A was extremely difficult for visitors.
   B confused even the staff.
   C involved understanding the symbols on a plan.
   D was regarded as a kind of game.

24 The writer characterises the productions of the film studio as

   A artistic creations.
   B exploiting the dissatisfaction of audiences.
   C escapist fiction.
   D reflecting the lives of ordinary people.

Film-makers

Almost everybody, it seems, wants to make a movie. Bookshops fill shelves with 'how-to' books about scriptwriting and film production. Fashionable universities offer courses. There are competitions offering the kind of hand-held camera that Robert Rodriguez used to make the film *El Mariachi*, which cost $7,000 to make and shot him from nowhere into the front line of American independent directors. If ever dreams came true, they did for Rodriguez – and ahead of schedule. Recalling his 23rd birthday in his book about his Mariachi adventures, he writes: 'Orson Welles made *Citizen Kane* when he was 25. Spielberg made *Jaws* at 26. So I've only got two or three years to make my breakthrough film.'

This was not always so. When the studios ruled, film-makers were expected to take time to mature. They worked behind the scenes, as editors, writers or cinematographers. They learnt the job directing low-budget westerns or supporting short films. John Huston was 35 when he made his first film, *The Maltese Falcon*. Fred Zinnemann, the director of *High Noon*, only got into his stride in his forties. But nowadays, without the support system of studios or television, aspiring film-makers are forced to be mavericks.

25 Why is Rodriguez used as an example in the first paragraph?

    A   He made a film on a deliberately restricted budget.
    B   His film has been compared to accepted masterpieces.
    C   He learnt effectively from what he had read.
    D   He showed how successful novice film-makers can be.

26 Under the studio system, film-makers

    A   could work from the start on individual projects.
    B   developed a range of professional skills.
    C   adopted a narrow technical approach.
    D   were always under pressure to succeed.

Part 3

You are going to read an extract from a novel. Seven paragraphs have been removed from the extract. Choose from the paragraphs **A–H** the one which fits each gap (**27–33**). There is one extra paragraph which you do not need to use.

Mark your answers **on the separate answer sheet**.

The Wrong Country

Uncle chose for them a package holiday at a very reasonable price: a flight from Gatwick Airport, twelve nights in Venice, the fairyland city, in the Pensione Concordia. When Keith and Dawne went together to the travel agency to make the booking, the counter clerk explained that the other members of that particular package were a school group from the south coast, all of them learning Italian. But something went wrong.

| 27 | |

At Gatwick they had handed their tickets to a girl in the yellow-and-red Your-Kind-of-Holiday uniform. She'd addressed them by name, had checked the details on their tickets and said that that was lovely. An hour later it had surprised them to hear elderly people on the plane talking in North of England accents. Keith said there must have been a cancellation, or possibly the Italian class was on a second plane.

| 28 | |

But the next morning, when it became apparent that they were being offered them for the duration of their holiday, they became alarmed.

'We have the lake, and the water birds,' the receptionist smilingly explained. 'And we may take the steamer to Interlaken.'

'An error has been made,' Keith informed the man, keeping the register of his voice even, for it was essential to be calm. He was aware of his wife's agitated breathing close beside him.

| 29 | |

'Your group is booked twelve nights in the Edelweiss Hotel. To make an alteration now, sir, if you have changed your minds –'

'We haven't changed our minds. There's been a mistake.'

The receptionist shook his head. He did not know about a mistake.

'The man who made the booking,' Dawne interrupted, 'was bald, with glasses and a moustache.' She gave the name of the travel agency in London.

| 30 | |

Again she gave the name of the travel agency and described the bald-headed counter clerk, mentioning his spectacles and his moustache. Keith interrupted her. 'It seems we got into the wrong group. We reported to the Your-Kind-of-Holiday girl and left it all to her.'

'We should have known when they weren't from Dover,' Dawne contributed. 'We heard them talking about Darlington.'

Keith made an impatient sound. He wished she'd leave the talking to him.

| 31 | |

'Now, what I am endeavouring to say to you good people is that all tickets and labels are naturally similar, the yellow with the two red bands.' Mrs Franks suddenly laughed. 'So if you simply followed other people with the yellow-and-red label you might imagine you could end up in a wildlife park! But of course,' she added soothingly, 'that couldn't happen in a million years.'

| 32 | |

'She seems quite kind,' Dawne whispered, 'that woman.' Keith wasn't listening. He tried to go over in his mind every single thing that had occurred: handing the girl the tickets, sitting down to wait, and then the girl leading the way to the plane, and then the pilot's voice welcoming them aboard, and the air hostess with the smooth black hair going round to see that everyone's seat belt was fastened.

| 33 | |

Keith walked out of the reception area and Dawne followed him. On the forecourt of the hotel they didn't

say to one another that there was an irony in the catastrophe that had occurred. On their first holiday since their honeymoon they'd landed themselves in a package tour of elderly people when the whole point of the holiday was to escape the needs and demands of the elderly. In his bossy way Uncle had said so himself when they'd tried to persuade him to accompany them.

A 'We noticed you at Gatwick,' Keith said. 'We knew you were in charge of things.'

'And I noticed *you*. I counted you, although I daresay you didn't see me doing that. Now, let me explain to you. There are many places Your-Kind-of-Holiday sends its clients to, many different holidays at different prices. There are, for instance, villa holidays for the adventurous under-thirty-fives. There are treks to Turkey, and treks for singles to the Himalayas.'

B 'We were meant to be in Venice. In the Pensione Concordia.'

'I do not know the name, sir. This is Switzerland.'

'A coach is to take us on. An official said so on the plane. She was here last night, that woman.'

C 'Nice to have some young people along,' an elderly man's voice interrupted Keith's thoughts. 'Nottage the name is.' The old man's wife was with him, both of them looking as if they were in their eighties. They'd slept like logs, she said, best night's sleep they'd had for years, which of course would be due to the lakeside air.

'That's nice,' Dawne said.

D The last of the elderly people slowly made their way from the dining room, saying good night as they went. A day would come, Dawne thought, when they would go to Venice on their own initiative, with people like the class from Dover. She imagined them in the Pensione Concordia, not one of them a day older than themselves.

E Either in the travel agency or at the check-in desk, or in some anonymous computer, a small calamity was conceived. Dawne and Keith ended up in a hotel called the Edelweiss, in Room 212, somewhere in Switzerland.

F 'We're not meant to be in Switzerland,' Keith doggedly persisted.

'Well, let's just see, shall we?'

Unexpectedly, Mrs Franks turned and went away, leaving them standing. The receptionist was no longer behind the reception desk. The sound of typing could be heard.

G 'Some problem, have we?' a woman said, beaming at Keith. She was the stout woman he had referred to as an official. They'd seen her talking to the yellow-and-red girl at Gatwick. On the plane she'd walked up and down the aisle, smiling at people.

'My name is Franks,' she was saying now. 'I'm married to the man with the bad leg.'

'Are you in charge, Mrs Franks?' Dawne enquired. 'Only we're in the wrong hotel.'

H They ordered two drinks, and then two more. 'The coach'll take us on,' a stout woman with spectacles announced when they touched down. 'Keep all together now.' There'd been no mention of an overnight stop in the brochure, but when the coach drew in at its destination, Keith explained that that was clearly what this was. As they stepped out of the coach it was close on midnight: fatigued and travel-stained, they did not feel like questioning their right to the beds they were offered.

Part 4

You are going to read an extract from a newspaper article. For questions **34–40**, choose the answer (**A**, **B**, **C** or **D**) which you think fits best according to the text.

Mark your answers **on the separate answer sheet**.

HE WAS A PEOPLE PERSON

American executives are adopting the polar explorer Ernest Shackleton as a model of good management.

Eluned Price reports.

Most people in Britain know who Sir Ernest Shackleton was and have a rough idea of what he did. America, however, has only just discovered him – although the *Wall Street Journal's* description of Shackleton earlier this year as 'an Antarctic explorer whose feats went all but unnoticed for most of the 20th century' is taking things too far. But now the Americans are making up for lost time with powerful enthusiasm. Biographies and accounts of the voyage of the *Endurance* are in production and are expected to spring off the shelves as fast as they are stacked; the American Museum of Natural History is mounting a grand exhibition; and Columbia Tristar is preparing a film based on Shackleton's life.

Some American managers have also adopted Shackleton as icon and exemplar. His self-appointed apostles recount the details of his deeds with awe; they extract lessons in leadership and communications as parables for spin doctors; and insiders refer to each other as 'speaking Shackleton'. The determined, resourceful Shackleton, with his reindeer sleeping bag (fur inside) and blubber-stove has become a model for modern management consultants.

Jim MacGregor, the managing partner of Abernathy MacGregor Frank in New York, took Shackleton for a role model years ago. His firm specialises in 'communication aspects of mergers and acquisitions and corporate crises'. Such as? Such as 'this firm's plant blew up' or 'half the workforce has to go'. While not forgetting that Shackleton served time in public relations for a Glasgow steel works, it may be a trifle difficult to spot instantly the relevance of eking out the last bit of albatross in sub-zero temperatures to putting a spin on a derivatives trading disaster for the Internet.

'Even if a company manages its crises beautifully, it can still do a lot of harm by communicating badly about what it's doing,' says MacGregor. 'Shackleton is a model for management because of his qualities as a leader and communicator. He had his values in order. He was at his best when he and those dependent on him had a great deal to lose – such as their lives. In some ways the most fascinating decision Shackleton made was to turn back when only 97 miles from the South Pole. That trip explained his credibility for the next one: the lives of his men were paramount.' This refers to Shackleton's expedition to reach the South Pole in 1908 when, 97 miles short of their objective, with unforeseen delays draining their supplies and limited time to get back to

their ship, Shackleton made the courageous and difficult decision to turn back.

In a crisis, says MacGregor, people want to know someone is in charge. Whereas now the tendency is for managers to duck and squirm, Shackleton was prepared to stand up and accept responsibility. His 1914 expedition was the one that became the stuff of legend. His ship, the *Endurance*, drifted for nine months in the pack ice and was finally crushed by ice floes. When it finally went down, Shackleton told his men, 'we should all eventually reach safety provided that you continue to do your utmost and to trust me'. From all the accounts and diaries the men kept, it is clear that there was never a time that the Boss was not in charge. 'Shackleton thought everything through, planned for every eventuality, kept his men continually informed and sought their opinions,' says MacGregor. 'He was adaptable, willing to let go when something was lost and start afresh. We've built an effective set of principles here that Shackleton illustrates. Clients can relate to his story without feeling they're being criticised.'

Shackleton believed that an explorer needs optimism, physical endurance and patience. 'One of the hardest things to do in desperate straits is nothing, especially in America, a culture that is fanatically opposed to letting time sort things out,' says MacGregor. 'If you buy bonds and guess wrong on the interest rates, you hang in there and eventually you'll get your money back. To "fix it" and sell up would mean a huge loss. Equally, don't be afraid to change your plans if they're not working. If a new product's a stinker, don't keep selling it.'

Shackleton led by example. On the voyage back from the *Endurance*, he noticed Hurley, the expedition photographer, gloveless. He forced his own on Hurley, saying if he didn't put them on he would throw them overboard. Someone else remembered him doing the same thing with a biscuit when they were near starving on the 1905 expedition: 'He said he'd leave it in the snow. Millions of pounds couldn't have bought that biscuit.' As Caroline Alexander, author of *Endurance*, the human account of that expedition, says: 'The public appetite for heroic endeavour is increasing. Shackleton exposes the fact that there is nothing heroic going on now. Everything else falls away and he is left standing, the genuine embodiment of the ideals that we are so wistful for nowadays.'

34   The writer says in the first paragraph that American enthusiasm for Shackleton reveals

    A   a certain amount of ignorance concerning his existing reputation.
    B   a tendency to exaggerate his achievements.
    C   the extent to which all explorers capture the public imagination.
    D   their strong desire to learn from the past.

35   In the second paragraph, the writer implies that some American managers

    A   have based their view of Shackleton on inaccurate information.
    B   regard Shackleton as a man who was ahead of his time.
    C   are mocked for their enthusiasm for Shackleton.
    D   misunderstand what Shackleton actually did.

36   What does the writer say in the third paragraph about using Shackleton as a role model?

    A   It is wise to take Shackleton's experiences outside the field of exploration into consideration.
    B   It is more appropriate in some business circumstances than in others.
    C   Connecting Shackleton's experiences with those of managers requires some imagination.
    D   People who do so often find it hard to explain why he is relevant.

37   According to Jim MacGregor, Shackleton's decision to end the 1908 expedition illustrates

    A   his ability to foresee the effect his actions would have on his reputation.
    B   his willingness to accept responsibility for mistakes that were not his fault.
    C   his ability to put the interests of others above his personal ambitions.
    D   his willingness to make decisions that others might criticise him for.

38   MacGregor uses Shackleton's behaviour during the 1914 expedition

    A   to teach managers the need to make decisions and then stick to them.
    B   to educate managers without implying that they themselves have shortcomings.
    C   to inspire managers by showing them how highly others think of them.
    D   to point out to managers the importance of letting others make decisions.

39   According to MacGregor, the culture in America is such that

    A   failing to take action when it is necessary is commonplace.
    B   managers frequently lack confidence in the decisions they make.
    C   managers impulsively change decisions they have made.
    D   taking action when it is inadvisable to do so is commonplace.

40   In the final paragraph, we are told that Shackleton's actions were of a kind that

    A   many people wish were more prevalent today.
    B   many people consider pleasantly eccentric these days.
    C   many people regard as no longer worthwhile these days.
    D   many people try to emulate these days.

PAPER 2   WRITING   (2 hours)

Part 1

You **must** answer this question. Write your answer in **300–350** words in an appropriate style.

1   *Lifestyles* magazine is intending to produce a special edition on consumer choice and how we decide what to buy. Readers are asked to submit articles expressing their own opinions in response to the comments below. You decide to write an article.

We buy things because we want them and not because we really need them.

When we go shopping we are all influenced by the media. They have a huge effect on dictating the latest trends and fashions.

I always have to have what my friends have.

Write your **article**.

Part 2

Write an answer to **one** of the questions **2–5** in this part. Write your answer in **300–350** words in an appropriate style.

---

2 A weekly magazine, *The Good Times*, has been publishing a series of readers' letters with the title *A day that changed my life for the better*. The Editor has asked people to send in letters to share their positive experiences with others. You decide to contribute.

Write your **letter**. Do not write any postal addresses.

3 An international magazine is conducting a survey amongst its readers into television viewing habits around the world. It has invited readers to send in reports on television in their own countries covering the following areas: the variety of programmes available, the popularity of particular kinds of programmes and the role television plays in people's lives.

Write your **report**.

4 A publisher is planning a book about festivals and customs from around the world. The publisher has asked people to submit proposals about what should be included on the festivals and customs which are unique to their own countries and which also maintain important traditions. You decide to submit a proposal to the publisher about your country.

Write your **proposal**.

5 Based on your reading of **one** of these books, write on **one** of the following:

(a) Brian Moore: *The Colour of Blood*
'In order to avoid another decade of violence in his country, Cardinal Bem has to rely on the help of people who would normally be his opponents.' Write an essay for your tutor describing how the Prime Minister (General Francis Urban) and the union organiser (Jop) help him and their reasons for doing so.

Write your **essay**.

(b) Anne Tyler: *The Accidental Tourist*
Your tutor has asked members of the class to review modern English or American novels which feature family life. Write a review of *The Accidental Tourist* in which you focus on the Leary family, showing how Macon Leary is influenced by and escapes from his family background.

Write your **review**.

(c) L.P. Hartley: *The Go-Between*
A literary magazine is running a series on the treatment of childhood in literature and has asked readers to send in articles on the topic. You decide to send in an article about the loss of childhood innocence in *The Go-Between*, describing how Leo's visit to Brandham Hall marked a significant turning point in his life.

Write your **article**.

PAPER 3   USE OF ENGLISH (1 hour 30 minutes)

Part 1

For questions **1–15**, read the text below and think of the word which best fits each space. Use only **one** word in each space. There is an example at the beginning **(0)**.

Write your answers in CAPITAL LETTERS **on the separate answer sheet**.

Example: | **0** | F | U | L | L | | | | | | | | | | | | | | | | |

Letter from a Genius

In 1912, the world's top mathematicians began to receive letters which were **(0)**....full.... of incredibly complex formulae. They came from Madras, in India, **(1)**............ a 23-year-old accounts clerk named Srinivasa Ramanujan had seemingly **(2)**............ up with hundreds of new solutions to known mathematical problems **(3)**............ any form of assistance or training.

For the most **(4)**............ , the professional mathematicians' response was the usual one **(5)**............ faced with eccentric letters: they consigned them straight **(6)**............ the bin. But in 1913, some reached G. H. Hardy, a leading authority in number theory at Cambridge University. He, too, initially dismissed the letters **(7)**............ the work of an eccentric, but unable to **(8)**............ them out of his head, he eventually subjected them to closer scrutiny. After a few hours, Hardy arrived **(9)**............ the conclusion that what he had **(10)**............ him was the work of a mathematical genius, a view confirmed by colleagues with **(11)**............ he shared his discovery.

Before very **(12)**............ , Ramanujan had received an invitation to Cambridge and, once there, he soon proved **(13)**............ worth. A fruitful collaboration with Hardy **(14)**............ in the opening up of vast areas of mathematical research, still being worked on to **(15)**............ day.

Part 2

For questions **16–25**, read the text below. Use the word given in capitals at the end of some of the lines to form a word that fits in the space in the same line. There is an example at the beginning **(0)**.

Write your answers in CAPITAL LETTERS **on the separate answer sheet**.

Example: | 0 | V | E | G | E | T | A | T | I | O | N | | | | | | | |

Lack of pastures new

Human activity made its mark on land use and **(0)**...*vegetation*... in coastal   **VEGETATE**
regions of southern Europe long before the first **(16)**............ holidays arrived.   **PACK**
By classical times, these areas had already seen extensive **(17)**............ by   **ERODE**
natural and human activity, and the process continues today.

The hospitable climate of the area, long appreciated in literature as well as
holiday brochures, produces seasonal variations in levels of soil **(18)**............   **MOIST**
and consequently in plant growth. In an area where **(19)**............ occur   **DRY**
frequently, there was a distinctive soil type at one time, with plants which had
adapted to it. Nowadays though, this soil cover is no longer in **(20)**............   **EXIST**
anywhere in the region.

The early years of the 1980s were **(21)**............ dry and this exacerbated   **EXCEPT**
problems brought about by the **(22)**............ growth of industry in rural areas   **SUBSTANCE**
and the intensification of agriculture. Pollution and insufficient water supplies
have become problems to which the landscape is increasingly **(23)**............ .   **SENSE**
The more recently this type of land has fallen out of use, the longer it takes for
plant cover to reestablish itself.

The European Union has set up a programme of **(24)**............ into land   **SEARCH**
degradation in southern Europe, involving forty-four universities in the
(25)............ of data which can be used to inform the policy decisions needed   **GATHER**
to deal with the issue.

Part 3

For questions **26–31**, think of **one** word only which can be used appropriately in all three sentences. Here is an example **(0)**.

Example:

0 Some of the tourists are hoping to get compensation for the poor state of the hotel, and I think they have a very ……………………… case.

There's no point in trying to wade across the river, the current is far too ……………………… .

If you're asking me which of the candidates should get the job, I'm afraid I don't have any ……………………… views either way.

| **0** | S | T | R | O | N | G | | | | | | | | | | |

Write **only** the missing word in CAPITAL LETTERS **on the separate answer sheet**.

---

26 There are several courses of action ……………………… to the government.

The job is still ……………………… if you're interested.

The two boxers looked at each other with ……………………… hostility.

27 From what the police spokesman said, we ……………………… that he'd been arrested.

The car rapidly ……………………… speed as it went down the hill.

The crowds ……………………… in the square to catch a glimpse of the film star.

28 The sports club is dependent on the local council for financial ……………………… .

Some famous celebrities have agreed to lend their ……………………… to the campaign.

Most tall buildings have steel frames in order to provide the necessary level of structural ……………………… .

29   When he goes to an Indian restaurant, Henry will always .... the hottest curry on the menu.

The ship's captain is going to .... the crew to cast off at dawn.

Writers should always .... their thoughts before putting pen to paper.

30   In Agatha Christie's crime stories, the detective always solves the .... of who the murderer is.

Angela invariably dresses in black and has an air of .... about her.

A .... bidder paid six million dollars for the Impressionist painting at yesterday's auction in New York.

31   I can't .... being with Julio when he's in a bad mood.

The fans said they would .... outside the stage door until the band appeared.

Do you think Sam will be able to .... the suspense of waiting for his present?

Part 4

For questions **32–39**, complete the second sentence so that it has a similar meaning to the first sentence, using the word given. **Do not change the word given.** You must use between **three** and **eight** words, including the word given.

Here is an example **(0)**.

Example:

0 Do you mind if I watch you while you paint?

objection

Do you .... you while you paint?

0	*have any objection to my watching*

Write **only** the missing words **on the separate answer sheet**.

---

32 There are fewer geese on the nature reserve than there were ten years ago.

declined

The number of geese on the nature reserve .... ten years.

33 I asked Sally to write us a short letter to let us know that she's arrived safely.

drop

I asked Sally .... to let us know that she's arrived safely.

34 Alan felt that it was unforgivable that Jane hadn't replied to his invitation.

failure

Alan felt that .... was unforgivable.

35 Marisa thought it would be possible for someone to turn the old vase into a plant pot.

made

Marisa thought that ………………………………………………………………… a plant pot.

36 Jeremy usually plays football on Saturdays.

habit

Jeremy is ………………………………………………………………… football on Saturdays.

37 When he was at his most successful, the president had enormous influence.

height

At ………………………………………………………………… , the president had enormous influence.

38 Shula is one of the few students to use the library extensively.

majority

Unlike ………………………………………………………………… extensive use of the library.

39 For me, his skill as a negotiator was most impressive.

how

I was most ………………………………………………………………… negotiator he was.

Part 5

For questions **40–44**, read the following texts on different branches of science. For questions **40–43**, answer with a word or short phrase. You do not need to write complete sentences. For question **44**, write a summary according to the instructions given.

Write your answers to questions **40–44 on the separate answer sheet**.

Science is concerned with the observation of the world around us and with devising plausible explanations for the events that are observed. There is nothing very mysterious about it, but its explanations have to be real explanations, and really convincing, and they are rarely final because each explanation raises new questions.

It is not until people working in a particular branch of science have accumulated large numbers of observations and have devised satisfactory explanations for them that they can start to make predictions. This takes time. Ecologists are still accumulating observations and devising explanations. Their science is growing rapidly, but it does not yet allow them to make many precise, reliable predictions. It is not their fault, or that of their science, but only that their discipline is very young.

line 9

This explains some of the worry and confusion that surrounds environmental issues. We are aware that problems exist, but uncertain about how serious they are or how to solve them without creating still more problems with our solutions. We need more information, and when scientists respond to environmental controversies by demanding more research they are not usually trying to evade the issue, or enhance their own careers. They really do need to know more. What ecologists have learned so far can be summed up very simply: the world is a great deal more complicated than anyone thought.

line 19

40   To what does 'This' refer in line 9?

   ....

41   Why does the writer say that scientists 'are not usually trying to evade the issue'? (line 19)

   ....

In recent times, systematic study of the Earth and its atmosphere is an activity that has accelerated and now there is a wide range of specialisms focusing on different aspects such as meteorology and geology that together can be called by the relatively new name of 'geoscience'. line 4

Throughout the centuries, there has been a growth in scientific knowledge and understanding of the air we breathe and the land that supports us. However, the 21st century will see science that is more structured and organised than formerly. Scientists observe, explain, predict and construct hypotheses to formalise this activity. Scientific advances occur when observations, measurements or other data cannot be explained by current theory. The advances usually involve increasing the complexity of the ideas, and the accompanying equations, to incorporate these 'exceptional' events. The physicist Richard Feynman likened this process to trying to work out the rules of chess from a small number of snapshots of the game. Despite this complexity, advances have been made, through thousands of individuals and teams observing, attempting to explain patterns, hypothesis-constructing, predicting, experimenting, data collecting and publishing in the areas of science where their natural curiosity and training have led them. In the future, it is likely that large teams with experts in different fields will collaborate to understand the complex interactions of the Earth's systems.

42   Which phrase in the first text is similar in meaning to 'the relatively new name' in the second text? (line 4)

   ....

43   What point is the writer making when he mentions what Richard Feynman said about analysing data?

   ....

44   In a paragraph of **50–70** words, summarise **in your own words as far as possible** what **both** texts say about why scientific knowledge constantly develops. Write your summary **on the separate answer sheet**.

PAPER 4   LISTENING (40 minutes approximately)

Part 1

You will hear four different extracts. For questions **1–8**, choose the answer (**A**, **B** or **C**) which fits best according to what you hear. There are two questions for each extract.

Extract One

You hear part of a radio programme about fame.

1 In the speaker's opinion, Hollywood stars of the past were

   A   remote from the public.
   B   famous for a variety of reasons.
   C   protected from scandal.

                         1

2 What does the speaker think celebrities nowadays should do?

   A   accept the temporary nature of fame
   B   exploit the potential of their situation
   C   avoid comparisons with younger rivals

                         2

Extract Two

You hear part of a radio programme about developments in instruments used in dance orchestras.

3 The first speaker explains that improvements to drumkits in the early twentieth century

   A   reflected the pace of musical change.
   B   were introduced by practising musicians.
   C   came about quite by accident.

                         3

4 According to Ralph Burton, his brother Vic was the first person to

   A   introduce a popular style of dance music.
   B   invent a new form of drumming equipment.
   C   change a particular instrument's use.

                         4

Extract Three

You hear part of an interview with the film critic Ian King, who is discussing a new film.

5 Ian thought that, in general, the special effects in the film

    A   were aimed at a wide age range.
    B   helped to speed up the narrative.
    C   were generally very creative.

        5

6 What did Ian dislike about the film?

    A   the development of the plot
    B   the way it was shot
    C   the quality of the acting

        6

Extract Four

You hear part of a football commentary on the radio.

7 The speaker says that Wyndham United won the match

    A   although they didn't deserve to.
    B   because of an early goal.
    C   because they were the fitter team.

        7

8 What does the speaker say about the players' behaviour during the match?

    A   He disapproves of the way it was handled.
    B   He thinks it got out of hand fairly soon after half-time.
    C   He thinks the referee intervened too hastily.

        8

Part 2

You will hear an interview with Peter Simon, a farmer from Scotland who keeps llamas, animals which are native to South America. For questions **9–17**, complete the sentences with a word or short phrase.

Before they became farmers, Peter and Ann worked in a family-run

	9

firm in London.

Ann uses the llama wool for making things like

	10

The nature of its coat ensures that the llama doesn't lose

	11

The persistent rain in Scotland caused

	12

disorders in the llamas.

Peter got round the problem caused by the rain by putting up

	13

for the llamas.

An unexpected result of having the llamas is that

	14

is now replacing other sorts of vegetation.

To supplement their income, the Simons have renovated a farm building for use as a

	15

For Peter, the most unexpected thing about the llamas is their

	16

Peter uses the word

	17

to describe the sound made by the llamas.

Part 3

You will hear a radio interview with Maureen Kemp, a ballet dancer. For questions **18–22**, choose the answer (**A**, **B**, **C** or **D**) which fits best according to what you hear.

18   Maureen got expert ballet training through

   A   a special teacher at her normal school.
   B   part-time classes at a famous school.
   C   going away to a special boarding school.
   D   extra classes at her first dancing school.

   [ ] 18

19   Her first experience of work with a choreographer

   A   was surprisingly unthreatening.
   B   occurred before she felt ready.
   C   increased her desire for success.
   D   was difficult because of the personal relationship.

   [ ] 19

20   Maureen finds working on a new piece

   A   physically demanding.
   B   emotionally exhausting.
   C   a nerve-racking experience.
   D   an unrewarding task.

   [ ] 20

21   Maureen does not want to create dances herself because

   A   she is too proud to accept criticism.
   B   she prefers other kinds of creative activity.
   C   she cannot find appropriate inspiration.
   D   she has difficulty developing her ideas fully.

   [ ] 21

22   Thinking about herself as a performer, Maureen

   A   loves the opportunity to show off.
   B   values the importance of technique.
   C   likes the chance to interact with the audience.
   D   draws inspiration from the roles she plays.

   [ ] 22

Part 4

You will hear part of a discussion in which two friends, Gordon and Martha, are discussing current issues in education. For questions **23–28**, decide whether the opinions are expressed by only one of the speakers, or whether the speakers agree.

Write   **G**   for Gordon,

          M   for Martha,

or   **B**   for Both, where they agree.

---

23   I think educating children at home is a very positive move.

         23

24   Socialising with other children is important.

         24

25   I believe that children have to learn to deal with difficulties.

         25

26   Alienated teenagers can cause a lot of problems in the community.

         26

27   It would be much easier to organise different activities for just a few children.

         27

28   Most new theories in education just lead to an increased burden for teachers.

         28

PAPER 5   SPEAKING (19 minutes)

There are two examiners. One (the Interlocutor) conducts the test, providing you with the necessary materials and explaining what you have to do. The other examiner (the Assessor) will be introduced to you, but then takes no further part in the interaction.

Part 1 (3 minutes)

The Interlocutor first asks you and your partner a few questions which focus on information about yourselves and personal opinions.

Part 2 (4 minutes)

In this part of the test you and your partner are asked to talk together. The Interlocutor places a set of pictures on the table in front of you. This stimulus provides the basis for a discussion. The Interlocutor first asks an introductory question which focuses on one or two of the pictures. After about a minute, the Interlocutor gives you both a decision-making task based on the same set of pictures.

The pictures for Part 2 are on pages C8–C9 of the colour section.

Part 3 (12 minutes)

You are each given the opportunity to talk for two minutes, to comment after your partner has spoken and to take part in a more general discussion.

The Interlocutor gives you a card with a question written on it and asks you to talk about it for two minutes. After you have spoken, your partner is first asked to comment and then the Interlocutor asks you both another question related to the topic on the card. This procedure is repeated, so that your partner receives a card and speaks for two minutes, you are given an opportunity to comment and a follow-up question is asked.

Finally, the Interlocutor asks some further questions, which leads to a discussion on a general theme related to the subjects already covered in Part 3.

The cards for Part 3 are on pages C2, C10 and C11 of the colour section.

Test 1 Key

Paper 1　Reading (1 hour 30 minutes)

Part 1　(one mark for each correct answer)

1 B　　2 D　　3 B　　4 C　　5 D　　6 A　　7 B　　8 D　　9 C
10 A　　11 B　　12 D　　13 B　　14 D　　15 C　　16 A　　17 C
18 B

Part 2　(two marks for each correct answer)

19 A　　20 C　　21 A　　22 B　　23 B　　24 A　　25 B　　26 D

Part 3　(two marks for each correct answer)

27 H　　28 F　　29 C　　30 A　　31 B　　32 E　　33 G

Part 4　(two marks for each correct answer)

34 C　　35 B　　36 B　　37 A　　38 B　　39 D　　40 D

Paper 2　Writing (2 hours)

Task-specific mark schemes

Question 1: Dilemmas

Content
Money and its relationship with happiness.

Major points for discussion:
* many people in the world are now richer than they were
* you don't need money to be happy

Further relevant point:
* most people in the world are not richer than they were

Range
Language for expressing and supporting opinions.

Appropriacy of register and format
Register appropriate to an essay.

Organisation and cohesion
Adequate use of paragraphing. Clear organisation of content with suitable introduction and conclusion.

Target reader
Tutor would be able to follow the discussion and understand the writer's point of view.

Question 2: Leisure Today

Content
Letter should explain what they collect, give details about how they collect and account for satisfaction derived from hobby.

Range
Language of description, narration and explanation.

Appropriacy of register and format
Consistently appropriate for letter to magazine.

Organisation and cohesion
Adequately organised in paragraphs. Clear introduction and conclusion.

Target reader
Would be interested in and informed about the hobby/collection described.

Question 3: The 50 Best Holiday Destinations

Content
Report should cover the following areas, where appropriate: accommodation, food, leisure facilities, places of interest and nightlife (some of these points may be combined). Should conclude with recommendation.

Range
Language of description and recommendation.

Appropriacy of register and format
Register appropriate to a report – may or may not include headings/sub-headings.

Organisation and cohesion
Clearly organised and paragraphed.

Target reader
Would be clearly informed about the destination.

Question 4: A Day That Changed My Life

Content
Article should describe an experience which had an important effect on candidate and say what the consequences were.

Range
Language of description and narration.

Appropriacy of register and format
Register appropriate for a magazine.

Organisation and cohesion
Clearly organised and paragraphed.

Target reader
Would be interested in the writer's experience.

Question 5(a): The Day of the Triffids

Content
<u>Exciting and entertaining:</u>
- the dramatic beginning
- throughout, the frightening encounters with Triffids
- the threat of the Triffids' increased powers (apparent hearing and learning)
- Bill's search for Josella
- the exciting escape at the end

<u>Believable?:</u>
- people's behaviour – how fear, etc. leads to cruelty and violence
- satellites – how the tragedy was of human making
- the threat of biological weapons
- the danger of genetic engineering

(Underlined points must be included – bulleted points are suggested relevant information.)

Range
Language of description, narration and evaluation.

Appropriacy of register and format
Consistently neutral/informal register suitable for fellow readers.

Organisation and cohesion
Well organised and paragraphed with an appropriate introduction and conclusion.

Target reader
Would have a clear idea of the book's plot and content and of the writer's view of the story.

Question 5(b): Our Man in Havana

Content
<u>Information about Beatrice's character and capabilities from:</u>
- information from HQ in London
- behaviour at Milly's party and assessment of herself as a 'crazy type'
- enthusiastic way she goes about organising the office but says 'what happens after work is real'
- after Raul's death, works hard at warning other agents, despite the bizarre circumstances
- after Hasselbacher's death, shows no surprise when Wormold confesses
- laughs about the drawings
- her final statement at HQ in London and ideas about the value and definition of 'loyalty'

(Underlined point must be included – bulleted points are suggested relevant information.)

Range
Language of description, narration and evaluation.

Appropriacy of register and format
Register consistent and appropriate for a general interest magazine.

Organisation and cohesion
Well organised and paragraphed.

Target reader
Would have some insight into Beatrice's character, the situations that faced her and how she dealt with them.

Question 5(c): The Accidental Tourist

Content
Information about Julian's character from:
- his background – boats, blazers, sunburnt nose
- his amusement at Macon
- his kindness over the turkey and Rose's distress
- his understanding of Macon's relationship with Muriel

Information about Julian's relationships from:
- his relationship with Rose – impressed by her qualities (care for the brothers, good organiser) – has great respect for her
- his relationship with Macon – he is amused by him, but understands him well – he accepts Macon's advice
- his relationship with the whole Leary family – he is intrigued by their unconventional ways and eager to join them as a family member

(Underlined points must be included – bulleted points are suggested relevant information.)

Range
Language of narration, description and evaluation.

Appropriacy of register and format
Consistent register, appropriate for letter to magazine.

Organisation and cohesion
Suitable introduction and conclusion, well organised and paragraphed.

Target reader
Would have a clear idea of the character and the part he plays in the novel.

Paper 3   Use of English (1 hour 30 minutes)

Part 1   (one mark for each correct answer)

1 come / learnt / learned   2 at   3 gone   4 then   5 nothing
6 from   7 such   8 again   9 with   10 wide   11 as
12 ourselves   13 rather   14 what   15 although / though / while / whilst

Part 2   (one mark for each correct answer)

16 drawbacks   17 autonomous   18 attendance   19 sufficiently
20 dreadfully   21 pressing   22 imaginative   23 expertise
24 immersion   25 invaluable

Part 3   (two marks for each correct answer)

26 reduced   **27** doubled   **28** complete   **29** heavy   **30** face
31 hand

Part 4   (one mark for each correct section)

32 was held up (1) + by / because of / due to / owing to / on account of / as a result of unforeseen (1)
33 wasn't / was not anything (else) (that) I could do (1) + except / other than / but / apart from (1) (NB: maximum of eight words)
34 without her brother / brother's (1) + having advised / advising her when / while (she was) (1) OR without the advice (1) + of her brother when / while / on (1)
35 subject to (1) + the council / council's agreeing / the council's agreement (1) OR the agreement of the council (1)
36 was her trainer's foreign accent (1) + which made / was making (1)
37 does Tim get (1) + the / any / an / opportunity to play (1) OR (any) opportunities to play (1) OR a / the / any chance to play / of playing (1)
38 drew our (1) + attention to (1)
39 are asked to / requested to (1) + remain seated / in their seats (1)

Part 5   (questions 40–43 two marks for each correct answer)

40 clown / infest / stench
41 inappropriate smells at the wrong time / smells getting mixed up
   paraphrase of 'plan going awry', e.g. things going wrong
42 because perfume houses / they rely (more / heavily) on science / technology / computers (to create a perfume)
43 paraphrase of 'makes visual the scent patterns', e.g. you can see smells
44 The paragraph should include the following points:
   i   confusion / mixing of smells
   ii   smells that are difficult to get rid of (when you want to)
   iii   some smells are unpleasant
   iv   nowadays, perfume companies can produce any kind of smell
   v   many new perfumes are very strange OR strange-smelling perfumes are now common

Paper 4   Listening (40 minutes approximately)

Part 1   (one mark for each correct answer)

1 C   **2** A   **3** A   **4** B   **5** B   **6** B   **7** C   **8** A

Part 2   (one mark for each correct answer)

9 distribution   **10** drainage (of the land)   **11** wings   **12** jewel(s) / gem(s)
13 blue-tailed   **14** large red   **15** still   **16** dawn / sunrise   **17** survey

Part 3   (one mark for each correct answer)

18 C   **19** A   **20** B   **21** C   **22** A

Part 4 (one mark for each correct answer)

23 T   **24** M   **25** B   **26** B   **27** M   **28** B

Transcript	*Certificate of Proficiency in English Listening Test. Test 1.*
	I'm going to give you the instructions for this test.
	I'll introduce each part of the test and give you time to look at the questions.
	At the start of each piece you'll hear this sound:
	tone
	You'll hear each piece twice.
	Remember, while you're listening, write your answers on the question paper.
	You'll have five minutes at the end of the test to copy your answers onto the separate answer sheet.
	There will now be a pause. Please ask any questions now, because you must not speak during the test.
	[pause]
PART 1	*Now open your question paper and look at Part One.*
	[pause]
	You'll hear four different extracts. For questions 1 to 8, choose the answer (A, B or C) which fits best according to what you hear. There are two questions for each extract.
Extract 1	[pause]
	tone

The robbery was captured on the bank's high-quality video cameras and they managed to get quite a few good shots of the robbers. Later, some people were arrested and I was sent some of their clothes and the bank film and asked, 'Can you see any of the clothing items on the film?' And I went through the film and found a number of good shots showing this one particular masked bank robber and his blue jeans.

Now people keep their jeans for a long period and with time they get these marks on them; spots where the blue dye gets rubbed away. Along the seams, this arrangement of bright spots and dark places where the dye hasn't been rubbed away looks like a computerised bar code. And for me it's like a fingerprint, because every one is slightly different.

And in the trial, the defence actually brought me in as an expert witness and, although the guy owned thirty-four pairs of jeans, we found the one from the film and that was enough to convict him.

[pause]

tone

[The recording is repeated.]

[pause]

113

Extract 2	[pause]
	tone
Interviewer:	This far we've discussed the effect and the experience of the students. Now what sort of effect have school trips had on you? What sort of responsibilities, for instance, have you had?
Teacher:	Well, obviously it's broadened my mind as well, but it certainly broadened my educational experience. It's certainly been the case that I realised in my particular role on these school trips, I'm not just the school teacher. It's very important that I still am considered to be the teacher and consider the educational values on this trip, as we have been talking about. But it's also the case that I suppose I've become a substitute parent as well. It's a very specific responsibility; you're with students twenty-four hours a day pretty much and obviously it's quite demanding and you need time to be their friend, at times to act as a parent. But I do think the teacher role is dominant otherwise the educational role of the trip perhaps might not be as reinforced as it should be.
Interviewer:	Well, thank you very much for sharing your experiences with us today.
	[pause]
	tone
	[The recording is repeated.]
	[pause]
Extract 3	[pause]
	tone
Interviewer:	Some critics talk about the explosion of musicals as what they loosely call 'dumbing down', but your argument, David, is that the effects have been much more subtle.
Playwright:	Well, I think the musical was the means by which, as in so many other aspects of British culture, politics and public policy, the eighties saw economics being exploited to gain political ends. In the arts there had been a 'conversation' for twenty years between the traditional 'high arts', the National Theatre, the BBC, the great orchestras and opera companies, and the provocative arts including the plays that bubbled up in the sixties which were politically and artistically radical. Now, in the eighties, there was a direct attack on the 'high arts' through the market place, through a mobilisation of the popular in the arts as a business, as arts pursuing a mass audience – the big musicals in fact. And the result of that ironically, it seems to me, was more or less the elimination of the provocative arts. That was the great sea change which had come about by the end of the eighties.
	[pause]
	tone
	[The recording is repeated.]
	[pause]

Extract 4   [pause]

                          tone

Amina: I have mixed feelings about the programme, actually, I think from a non-twin perspective it was reasonably informative from a scientific point of view, to see how things happen and why you get different types of twins. But from a twin perspective, there were a few things that I was a bit disgruntled about, if you like, certain sweeping statements that I found difficult to understand. For example, when the programme showed us newborn twin girls and Professor Graham implying that what they really would have to cope with in the future was growing up as identical twins.

Fatma: Hmm. I think the underlying assumption is this idea of individuality, which always seems to be emphasised when you see any programmes to do with twins, and the view that there's something wrong if you're not trying to be so-called 'individual'. I think this is quite a western concept and, certainly for us, coming from an Indian background, it was quite alien. Which is not to say, of course, that we don't in fact possess quite distinct personality traits…

Amina: …which complement each other in so many ways.

Fatma: True.

                          [pause]

                          tone

                          [The recording is repeated.]

                          That's the end of Part One.

                          Now turn to Part Two.

                          [pause]

PART 2   *You will hear a talk given by a naturalist who is interested in a type of insect called the damselfly. For questions 9 to 17, complete the sentences with a word or short phrase.*

                          You now have forty-five seconds in which to read Part Two.

                          [pause]

                          tone

                          Good evening. Now you may think that looking into the murky depths of a muddy pond doesn't sound much like fun. But I have many happy childhood memories of doing just that, as I went hunting for the insects that have always fascinated me. For it is in surroundings like these that you can find one of the fastest and oldest species of insect in the world, the dragonfly, and its elusive but beautiful smaller cousin, the damselfly.

                          The speed of these insects is estimated to vary from 35 to 60 miles per hour, and fossilised remains show them to have been in existence 300 million years ago. But apart from that, relatively little is known about these creatures, particularly the damselfly, the abundance and distribution of which in Britain can only be guessed at.

                          115

What is known is that changes to the rural landscape have been affecting the population of these charming creatures over recent decades. Developments such as land drainage and the filling-in of ponds have certainly taken their toll, but exactly how much is difficult to assess. And this is where you come in, because conservation organisations desperately need your help in locating the remaining damselfly habitats.

So, how do you go about this? Well, first of all, when you make what you think is a sighting of a damselfly, it is necessary to make a positive identification. The insect is similar to its close relation the dragonfly, but differs in several respects. Firstly, the dragonfly has a rapid, strong flight, while its damsel cousin is delicate with frail wings and is therefore relatively weak in flight. Secondly, you should try to observe the insect when it is at rest. When the dragonfly is not flying, its wings are held out at right angles to its body. This is in direct contrast to the damselfly which holds its wings over its body so that they are touching each other, rather like a butterfly. I would like to emphasise that this is a stronger distinguishing feature than, say, the eyes or body.

As regards colouring, damselflies can be blue, red or green, but these are not ordinary colours, there's nothing muted about them. They are vivid and they sparkle in the sunlight like jewels as the insects dart about from place to place. And some of them have names that reflect this; the Emerald damselfly and the Azure damselfly, both of which may be spotted locally. It is, however, the more prosaically named Blue-tailed damselfly that is actually the most frequently sighted in the region. Whilst others you might see include the Common Blue damselfly, which is not as common as its name suggests, and the Large Red damselfly which is thought almost to have died out locally, and so if you should get a sighting of that one we'd certainly be interested in hearing about it.

Now, where and when to look for them? Well, not surprisingly the summer months are best, from May onwards, but not much after August. It is a relatively short season. And you need to be looking in areas where there is water. Although you may find them in gardens, especially near slow-moving streams, damselflies really thrive in the vegetation that is found in and around still water. It is here that they find the smaller flying insects which are their prey and it is also here that they lay their eggs below the surface of the water. In terms of the best time of day, avoid the afternoon and evenings because these insects are definitely early-risers. The ideal time to catch up with them is soon after dawn.

And so please, if you see damselflies, and if you find them as captivating as I do, then please don't just walk away and forget them. The Conservation Trust is keen to produce a survey of the remaining sites that provide a habitat and so put pressure on the authorities to preserve them for future generations, so do let them know what you see and where you see it.

[pause]

Now you'll hear Part Two again.

tone

[The recording is repeated.]

[pause]

That's the end of Part Two.

Now turn to Part Three.

[pause]

PART 3   *You will hear a radio interview with the artist Madeline Knowles. For questions 18 to 22, choose the answer (A, B, C or D) which fits best according to what you hear.*

You now have one minute in which to look at Part Three.

[pause]

tone

Presenter: Her paintings reflect the peaceful nature of country life, a vase of pansies or roses, a few buttercups or some bluebells. A new book, *The Art of Madeline Knowles*, has been published this week to coincide with her 75th birthday, and she currently has exhibitions in London and Cardiff. Madeline, why do you usually paint very peaceful subjects rather than the harsher realities of life?

Madeline: Well, I think the thing about plants, actually, is that they're quite wonderful; they're absolutely adapted to survival and I think that what we see as grace and beauty is actually strength. When I'm painting flowers, I'm looking for their inner strength and wanting to show it. It isn't, for me, done in order to be peaceful, it's done in order to discover that something inside which keeps them going.

Presenter: But is art, then, just to please the eye and calm the nerves, because that's how we respond to it, isn't it?

Madeline: I think mankind has always needed art; for magic, for celebration, for embellishment, and artists meanwhile have been trying to produce some sort of sense out of this funny old world in which we exist. And I think artists today, we're still trying to find that order and show it to people when we paint.

Presenter: So, you don't approve of what's called the modern movement?

Madeline: I think my kind of painting is part of the modern movement, but it's a description that gets overused and often in a misleading fashion. For example, those artists at the so-called 'cutting edge' are only one very small part of it which gets a lot of attention in the media and elsewhere.

Presenter: Now, you began as a designer of textiles rather than a painter. Why did you change, was it very important to you to paint?

Madeline: Well, I jumped into it really. I hadn't sought the change at all. I was teaching drawing at the time, as well as doing my own design work. And I was suddenly asked for some reason, staff shortages or something, to do the painting classes with the students as well. So, it made me shift, I had to get a box of paints and go out and paint myself, in order to feel prepared. And, of course, I found it such a… I don't know, almost, sort of, an enormous relief, that I haven't looked back since.

Presenter: And these days you teach just the one rather famous person, I believe. What was it in your work that appealed particularly to Andy Benson, the rock star?

Madeline: Well, I think he saw a little painting of mine in an exhibition, it had a pathway running up to a village, I think, but it was the image that caught his attention because when I got to his house, I was early, and so I was waiting in the sitting room for a quarter of an hour or so, and I looked out of the window and saw that he was outside creating a path with stones, and it struck me that it must have been that image which had appealed to him. I understand that on seeing my picture, he'd said, 'Oh, I'd like my garden painted like that.'

Presenter:	And initially that's what you were invited to do, of course.
Madeline:	That's right. But then later he did ask me for advice about his own paintings.
Presenter:	Which you gave?
Madeline:	Oh yes, we had a go through them because he was working for an exhibition the following year.
Presenter:	And your advice was?
Madeline:	Oh, it was the usual art school advice about big shapes and little shapes. Quite a formal discussion. It wasn't about how he felt about the landscapes that he was doing, that's for him. I treat him just like an art school student really.
Presenter:	Madeline Knowles, thank you very much for joining me today.
Madeline:	Thank you.

[pause]

Now you'll hear Part Three again.

tone

[The recording is repeated.]

[pause]

That's the end of Part Three.

Now turn to Part Four.

[pause]

PART 4   *You will hear a discussion on the radio on the subject of rock festivals. For questions 23 to 28, decide whether the opinions are expressed by only one of the speakers, or whether the speakers agree. Write T for Tim, M for Maria or B for both, where they agree.*

You now have thirty seconds in which to look at Part Four.

[pause]

tone

Presenter:	Earlier today, Tim Brown, our environment correspondent, spoke to Maria Taylor of *Environment Now*.
Tim:	The open season on rock festivals is about to start unleashing joy and anguish side by side all over the country. If you're heading off towards the three-day packed programme at Greenwood this weekend, then you probably love them. If you live within the area, you're probably battening down the hatches in fear and trepidation of some of the chaos that's about to descend on your neighbourhood. But rock festivals may not only bombard your ears, they can also affect the environment, as thousands of enthusiastic revellers converge on one venue.
Maria:	Well, Tim, I think we have to be careful not to fall into the trap of assuming that all festivals cause exactly the same problems. I think a rural festival – such as Greenwood – that's almost bound to generate traffic jams and clog up the winding lanes of the countryside, but at least it's not near to a major centre of population, so to that extent the impact's limited.
Tim:	But the traffic generation associated with these festivals is a cause for concern. Car use is far too great and often can't be accommodated within the rural road network around many of these sites.

Maria:	Well, compare it, say, with the two Peter Storm concerts in July, one's at The GP Centre, and the other's at the Sampson Bowl. Now both sites are much more accessible by public transport, but they are also much closer to urban centres and the impact is far greater.
Tim:	Now, the noise and other disturbance associated with festivals can sometimes be unacceptable for not just local residents but people living in the wider vicinity, can't it?
Maria:	And then you get the sort of thing that happened at the Tandem Festival at Lockley last year.
Tim:	Yes, I heard about that. It was a shambles, wasn't it?
Maria:	Mmm, there was gridlock outside; it looks as if 70,000 tickets were issued for a site which was only licensed for half that number. Concert-goers there ended up waiting in jams for up to 16 hours before getting in, but anyone could have seen that coming.
Tim:	No shocks there, because as I recall there was only one entrance and exit to the site. But I gather that access is being improved there for this year's event.
Maria:	Apparently. But there are still issues to be resolved there. The temporary and not so temporary things that are erected on the festival sites, which can have an intrusive impact on the landscape in the longer term…
Tim:	…and if they're not taken down after the event, they're unsightly, aren't they? Now there's other pollution as well, not to put too fine a point on it, rubbish, that has an effect, isn't there?
Maria:	Hmm, the organisers at Greenwood have become increasingly aware of their environmental obligations. They weren't always that bothered but now it's certainly a lot better in that way than the other big festivals.
Tim:	But at the same time it's a massive commercial event, like they all are…
Maria:	It's not aiming to make a loss, any more than the others do, let's put it that way. But the changes that the organisers have introduced are helping and they're certainly being able to recycle more of the waste each year and that's the direction they're moving in.

[pause]

Now you'll hear Part Four again.

tone

[The recording is repeated.]

[pause]

That's the end of Part Four.

There will now be a pause of five minutes for you to copy your answers onto the separate answer sheet. Be sure to follow the numbering of all the questions.

Note: Teacher, stop the recording here and time five minutes. Remind students when there is **one** minute remaining.

[pause]

That's the end of the test. Please stop now. Your supervisor will now collect all the question papers and answer sheets.

Test 2 Key

Paper 1   Reading (1 hour 30 minutes)

Part 1   (one mark for each correct answer)
1 D   2 A   3 C   4 A   5 D   6 B   7 A   8 B   9 C
10 A   11 C   12 A   13 A   14 B   15 B   16 C   17 B
18 D

Part 2   (two marks for each correct answer)
19 B   20 D   21 B   22 C   23 C   24 A   25 C   26 A

Part 3   (two marks for each correct answer)
27 H   28 F   29 B   30 D   31 A   32 G   33 E

Part 4   (two marks for each correct answer)
34 C   35 A   36 D   37 D   38 A   39 B   40 B

Paper 2   Writing (2 hours)

Task-specific mark schemes

Question 1: Children's freedom

Content
Degree of freedom given to children.

Major points for discussion:
- children gain from being given freedom
- it is irresponsible to give young people freedom

Further relevant point:
- many children get freedom from an early age

Range
Language for expressing and supporting opinions.

Appropriacy of register and format
Consistently appropriate for letter to newspaper.

Organisation and cohesion
Adequately organised in paragraphs. Clear introduction and conclusion.
Introductory and concluding conventions.

Target reader
Would understand writer's opinions.

Question 2: Soap operas

Content
Review of popular soap opera. Explanation of popularity of soap operas in general.

Range
Language of description and explanation.

Appropriacy of register and format
Register appropriate for piece of writing for tutor.

Organisation and cohesion
Clearly organised and paragraphed. Clear linkage between specific review and general discussion of soap operas.

Target reader
Would be informed about specific soap opera and writer's views on the popularity of soap operas.

Question 3: A Museum or Exhibition

Content
Brief description of museum or exhibition. Focus on one exhibit and reasons for choice of that exhibit.

Range
Language of description, explanation and evaluation.

Appropriacy of register and format
Register appropriate for article in college magazine.

Organisation and cohesion
Clearly organised and paragraphed. Clear linkage between two parts of question.

Target reader
Would be informed about museum or exhibition. Would be interested in exhibit described.

Question 4: Tourism and the Local Environment

Content
Proposal on ways of encouraging tourists to continue visiting the writer's area. Awareness of threat to the environment.

Range
Language of description and making recommendations.

Appropriacy of register and format
Proposal format – probably with section headings/sub-headings. Register appropriate to a formal working relationship.

Organisation and cohesion
Well-structured proposal with clear sections. Presentation of ideas in coherent prose. Appropriate use of linking and paragraphing.

Target reader
Would understand the issues and what writer is proposing.

Question 5(a): The Day of the Triffids

Content

<u>Excitement in episodes:</u>
- dramatic beginning to novel
- various occasions when Triffids attack
- descriptions of violence and anarchy as society breaks down
- continuing suspense of Bill's search for Josella
- final dramatic escape from Shirning

<u>Interest in relationships:</u>
- Bill and Josella – Bill's search defines the plot in the early stages
- Bill and Coker
- Bill and Susan
- Various brief but relevant encounters, e.g. the unnamed blind girl
- Relationship/conflict between the different groups with different ideas of how to reorganise society

(Underlined points must be included – bulleted points are suggested relevant information.)

Range

Language of description and narration, analysis and evaluation.

Appropriacy of register and format

Register and format appropriate to a report, possibly with headings or sub-headings. Consistent register.

Organisation and cohesion

Appropriate introduction, reason for writing and conclusion. Well-organised report with clear presentation of ideas. Adequate use of paragraphing and linking.

Target reader

Would be well informed about the book and its suitability for radio.

Question 5(b): Our Man in Havana

Content

<u>Circumstances leading to the meeting of Wormold and Beatrice and aspects of the characters of Wormold and Beatrice:</u>
- brief outline of each character's role
- description of Milly's birthday party – where first meeting takes place
- information about Wormold's character – as salesman, as Milly's father, as Hasselbacher's friend; his attitude to spying
- information about Beatrice – gained from first episode in London, behaviour at the birthday party, attitude to her husband, way she adapts to the job as Wormold's secretary
- as the story develops – their attitudes to the business of spying and their ideas and beliefs about loyalty are developed and defined

(Underlined points must be included – bulleted points are suggested relevant information.)

Range

Language of description, narration and evaluation.

Appropriacy of register and format
Consistent register for article suitable for inclusion in magazine.

Organisation and cohesion
Suitable introduction – reason for writing. Well organised, moving from description/narration to evaluation/analysis.

Target reader
Would have some understanding of the characters and how their relationship develops.

Question 5(c): The Accidental Tourist

Content
Macon's character:
- evidence from the way he organises his life
- the way he writes about travel
- the way he controls emotions and lets himself be controlled by what happens to him

Muriel's character:
- chaotic lifestyle
- chaotic house, but full of people
- over-protective and careful about Alexander
- open about her emotions

(Underlined points must be included – bulleted points are suggested relevant information.)

Range
Language of discussion, narration and evaluation.

Appropriacy of register and format
Consistent and appropriate for essay for tutor.

Organisation and cohesion
Clear presentation of ideas; well organised and paragraphed.

Target reader
Would have a clear understanding of the writer's view.

Paper 3   Use of English (1 hour 30 minutes)

Part 1   (one mark for each correct answer)

1 fewer   2 far   3 very   4 though / although / while / whilst   5 too
6 his   7 on / upon   8 to   9 with   10 all
11 little / no / nothing   12 did   13 its   14 such   15 these / those

Part 2   (one mark for each correct answer)

16 intervention   17 additional   18 procedure   19 notoriously
20 ascertain   21 inconclusive   22 researchers   23 rigorous
24 rainfall   25 findings

Part 3   (two marks for each correct answer)

26 imitation   **27** apply   **28** term   **29** human   **30** review
31 seek

Part 4   (one mark for each correct section)

32 a good / great deal more (1) + skill than (1)
33 did not / didn't go (1) + down (so / particularly / all that / very) (1)
34 explanation (1) + was ever given (1) OR explanations (1) + were ever given (1)
35 resignation / resigning / decision to resign came (1) + as a (total / complete) surprise / shock to (1)
36 on the verge (1) + of leaving / going out of (1)
37 to extend his / her (1) + stay at the hotel by (1)
38 did not / didn't have any / had no intention (1) + of interrupting (1)
39 unlike him (1) + to be / arrive / come / turn up / late (1) OR not to be in / on time (1)

Part 5   (questions 40–43 two marks for each correct answer)

40 (They, and all the other characters, are) stock figures
41 stories are (only) believed because details / information (e.g. times and places) are not known / not specified / left vague OR stories would not be believed if details / information (e.g. times and places) were known / specified
42 adults say that (all) people are good but children know that they (themselves) are not always good OR (because) children know they behave differently from how they are told they should behave
43 (what) adults / parents / society / community (say / think / believe) OR the (leading) beliefs / values / customs (of the time)
44 The paragraph should include the following points:
   i   the stories include practical details
   ii   the virtues and rewards in the stories are real
   iii   they reflect the social conditions / details of the times when the stories were first told
   iv   the stories show that life has problems
   v   with effort obstacles / difficulties can be overcome

Paper 4   Listening (40 minutes approximately)

Part 1   (one mark for each correct answer)

1 B   **2** A   **3** B   **4** C   **5** B   **6** A   **7** B   **8** C

Part 2   (one mark for each correct answer)

9 (different) colour(s) / color(s)   **10** (huge) barrel   **11** (sponge)(-)farming
12 dry / dried / dried(-)out (specimens / sponges)   **13** horn   **14** love and commitment (in either order)   **15** (as) hard as (a) rock / rock(-)hard NOT hard alone   **16** cell(-)to(-)cell   **17** (new) (kinds of / types of) drug(s) / medicine(s)

Part 3   (one mark for each correct answer)
18 D   **19** B   **20** C   **21** D   **22** A

Part 4   (one mark for each correct answer)
23 V   **24** B   **25** T   **26** B   **27** B   **28** T

Transcript   *Certificate of Proficiency in English Listening Test. Test 2.*

I'm going to give you the instructions for this test.

I'll introduce each part of the test and give you time to look at the questions.

At the start of each piece you'll hear this sound:

tone

You'll hear each piece twice.

Remember, while you're listening, write your answers on the question paper.

You'll have five minutes at the end of the test to copy your answers onto the separate answer sheet.

There will now be a pause. Please ask any questions now, because you must not speak during the test.

[pause]

PART 1   *Now open your question paper and look at Part One.*

[pause]

You'll hear four different extracts. For questions 1 to 8, choose the answer (A, B or C) which fits best according to what you hear. There are two questions for each extract.

Extract 1   [pause]

tone

The latest wave of worry started in the 1960s and there's been a proliferation of societies for the preservation of pure English ever since. And, you know, when all else fails, when they've got nowhere with teachers and public figures and so on, these people would write to us. And I drew the short straw of having to deal with all those letters complaining about the language. These ranged from those drawing our attention to our own piddling misprints, to those vilifying the general use of vogue words such as 'ongoing' or 'scenario', or whatever, in the media, and those cataloguing the alleged mispronunciation of newsreaders, this latter being a real obsession with some of the most persistent correspondents.

[pause]

tone

[The recording is repeated.]

[pause]

Extract 2	[pause]
	tone
Interviewer:	So, you're finished with competitive skating, and you're going to carry on choreographing ice shows, what else?
Skater:	Well, I'm only forty-two, full of energy.
Interviewer:	And I hear you've taken to the boards?
Skater:	I love the stage; there's something about the immediacy of being on stage with an audience that's ten metres away from you as opposed to the distance in an ice arena. And I've been fortunate enough not only to have skated on a theatrical stage and have the audience there but also to have danced in some of the great shows, *Cats*, *Rocky Horror*.
Interviewer:	But when you dance, don't you miss the skates terribly?
Skater:	I don't miss the skates, but in rehearsals, it did take some getting used to. In ice skating, you take a few steps and you've travelled 20 metres at high speed. I was tenpin bowling with the rest of the cast; I was making my steps and banging into other people, then I realised you can do all this great choreography and move nowhere.

[pause]

tone

[The recording is repeated.]

[pause]

Extract 3	[pause]
	tone

I thought the film was rather limp and morose. A rather low-powered film and unfortunately not a very good adaptation of the novel. I think part of the problem is that this particular novelist is not a very filmic writer on many occasions. Most of the pleasures one gets from reading him are pleasures of language ... he's very playful, he's very witty with language, but the message goes straight from the eye to the brain. You don't need pretty pictures to intervene. So wisely, on the one hand, the film-makers have skipped a lot of the verbal playfulness, but what they're left with is a rather pedestrian story firmly set in the seventies examining the issue of conformity and it all seems to have lost its relevance. The other thing which is lost in the translation is that the heroes, Chris and Tony, are very clever boys; they're very bright and witty, but in the film Chris is a rather pedestrian character. Tony, who in the book is a rather exotic character, whose sense of otherness Chris wants to emulate, just comes across as a bit of a thug and totally unappealing.

[pause]

tone

[The recording is repeated.]

[pause]

| Extract 4 | [pause] |
| | tone |

Interviewer:	Dr Brown, we do like to have routines, don't we?
Dr Brown:	Well, I think there are certain people who prefer to have routines and I'd classify them in two groups: those that are a bit more inflexible in their own normal personality, and they perceive change as an annoyance. And the other big group would be those who have a diurnal variation in their mood and their intellectual processes, in the sense that they are slower starters in the morning, they prefer a slower routine, and change impinges on them; it kind of throws them off balance. And for them, an early morning routine is economical of effort in all sorts of ways.
Interviewer:	Many things become central to our lives, don't they? The morning newspaper…
Dr Brown:	Exactly. And many people find changes difficult. So it's really important how change is managed. You know, some people in industry just spring things on their staff. They bring in a lot of new changes without paving the way, and the workers feel demoralised because they're not taken on board first, so they've got no incentive to cooperate.

[pause]

tone

[The recording is repeated.]

That's the end of Part One.

Now turn to Part Two.

[pause]

PART 2

You will hear part of a radio programme about creatures which live in the sea. This part of the programme is about sponges. For questions 9 to 17, complete the sentences with a word or short phrase.

You now have forty-five seconds in which to look at Part Two.

[pause]

tone

Well, here we are in front of an enormous aquarium full of sponges. As you can see, sponges are incredibly beautiful and incredibly diverse. When people think of a sponge there's often not much colour to them, but those sponges are actually just the skeleton of the living sponge. They come in all different colours from lavender to brilliant pinks and blues and yellows, which is not at all what a lot of people expect. They're from just millimetres in size to – to three metres in width. They come in anything from a thin encrusting on rocks to something that looks like a huge barrel. I study sponges that are mainly marine sponges, but sponges are found in fresh water too, as well as in marine waters, cold, temperate, polar, arctic waters. They're everywhere, in waters all over the world.

The most interesting thing about sponges, I think, is that they have incredible regenerative properties. For example, if you take a small piece of sponge from the individual, the individual closes up that gap and regenerates the tissue. So this is the principle behind sponge farming. They will take small pieces or cut one individual into several different pieces, then tie those pieces onto a string, leave them out in the ocean and the sponge will regenerate a whole new individual.

Now we're down in the basement of the museum and this room with all these boxes, this is where we hold all our dry specimens of sponges and here at the Natural History Museum we have about a quarter of a million specimens. So if we look in this box here… yes, this box represents one class of sponges.

Sponges are composed of three different classes. And these are known as 'glass' sponges. As you can see, they're very fine and the skeleton's actually made of silicone dioxide or glass. They're a kind of horn shape and this sponge in particular is significant in Japanese weddings. This species always harbours small shrimps, and they're usually found in pairs. The small shrimps get trapped inside the sponge. They can actually live and grow in here, and this is given as a symbol in the marriage ceremony of love and commitment. These two shrimps are bound in this sponge forever.

Ah! Here's something excellent. Yes, look in this box here. This is a sponge, a demonstration sponge, you see it's on a wooden pedestal. Well, probably because it's been on show in the galleries. While some of the sponge specimens are soft and pliable, this sponge, however, is as hard as rock.

Now, going back to what I said earlier, I'm really interested in how we can use sponges to help us understand human diseases. For example, a classic experiment was performed where they took a sponge and pushed it through a cheesecloth so that all the sponge cells were separated and put in an aquarium. And after a period of time, these separate sponge cells actually reconstituted and formed the same organism again. So that cell-to-cell interaction, as we call it, is incredibly important and the researchers are looking at that and ways they can apply that to human needs. If they can understand this process, then possibly they can understand why in some cases somebody may develop a certain type of disease when their cell growth goes wrong.

The most significant research that is done on sponges from the point of view of human needs is in the manufacture of new kinds of drugs. You see, sponges are sessile organisms which means they can't actually move…

[pause]

Now you'll hear Part Two again.

tone

[The recording is repeated.]

[pause]

That's the end of Part Two.

Now turn to Part Three.

[pause]

PART 3   *You will hear part of a radio programme in which guidebooks are discussed. For questions 18 to 22, choose the answer (A, B, C or D) which fits best according to what you hear.*

You now have one minute in which to look at Part Three.

[pause]

tone

Presenter: Well, in front of me today I have a tableload of Wayfarer Guides and Blueprint Guides and Meander Guides to at least two dozen different destinations. And with me to assess their qualities I have John Lock, the legendary travel editor and publisher. John, why is there such a glut of travel guides?

John: Well, I think partly it should be said that it's a commercial decision by publishers because just so many more people are travelling and so many more people are adventurous, and even… you notice… with… um… much older people who might have gone and stayed at the seaside in Britain and now they're boasting about having been in exotic, distant parts of the world. And so huge tracts of the world just weren't covered by guidebooks, and now they are.

Presenter: So what are the things you look for in a modern guide?

John: Rule number one, I think, with any guidebook is look and see if it's written by a human being, and these series, you notice, there's no name attached to them, and so there's nobody's pride at stake to make sure that the information is accurate, that the index works and everything else.

Presenter: There are a number of guides out now which are absolutely stuffed with photographs and pictures and so on, there's the Wayfarer Guides, their guide to Spain is about, sort of, what, 600 pages long, it costs 20 quid and every page is crammed with photographs and maps and what have you in full colour…

John: …Why have all these huge pictures all the way through? It's a cynical publishing ploy because they think people will buy things with colour pictures, which isn't necessarily the case because one problem is, anything with colour pictures is going to weigh a lot more…

Presenter: Sure.

John: …because you have to have suitable paper. Two, it takes up room that could be used for valuable information… and I'm sure that one's missing a lot of valuable information. What I would do in a bookshop if I had this in my hand, I would go to another book about Spain and I would look up some specific, comparatively minor topic and then see how these books dealt with it. One example is, in Italy, in Florence, one of the most enjoyable sights, I think, is the Monastery of San Marco…

Presenter: That's a lovely place…

John: …exactly, and I once tested the various guidebooks on this and it was quite extraordinary the difference in both content and tone, and tone is of course important. Sometimes it was a much smaller book that really told you exactly what you wanted to know about it.

Presenter: The Blueprint Guides, I notice, pride themselves on gradually evolving and having more bits of information every year from more experts. The only trouble with them is, as with many other guidebooks, they try to establish a distinction between kind of the ordinary narrative of where to stay and what this region is like and sort of kind of gobbets of history or topography, which they represent in tiny little teeny weeny four-point type. And opening the *Blueprint Guide to Southern Italy* almost anywhere, one reads this sort of thing: 'The second south chapel contains a good 18th century Baroque altar and a 16th century tomb…' and blah blah blah it goes on and on like that. The curious thing is, it gives the impression of being kind of murmured because it's in this tiny little type as if some ancient academic person is muttering away to himself. Is there a sense in which one had to be kind of sparing with information rather than throwing everything at the reader?

John: I think I would possibly disagree with you a bit, in that I think there are two types of thing, one is… I would agree in that one does want more discursive chat, interesting stuff about how people are living in a place, the background of their lives, what they think of the government. However, sometimes when you come to a really stunning sight or building or whatever, you slow down to an entirely different pace and you do want some very hard, reliable detail.

Presenter: John Lock, a guidebook connoisseur. Now when you're travelling, you…

[pause]

Now you'll hear Part Three again.

tone

[The recording is repeated.]

[pause]

That's the end of Part Three.

Now turn to Part Four.

[pause]

PART 4   *You will hear two friends, Tim and Vera, discussing a concert which was held in the dark. For questions 23 to 28, decide whether the opinions are expressed by only one of the speakers, or whether the speakers agree. Write T for Tim, V for Vera, or B for both, where they agree.*

You now have thirty seconds in which to look at Part Four.

[pause]

tone

Tim: Well, that was certainly a different experience, all of us sitting in the dark in a concert hall listening to music. What did you make of it, Vera?

Vera: What I found really interesting was I was totally focused on the music for once and not busy glancing around at who was sitting next to me or admiring the hairstyle of the person in front. And I kind of heard the music like I'd never heard it before; it was a different experience.

Tim: Well, I started wondering about how I was going to listen to the music when I got home and was trying to make myself more aware of the other senses I was going to use to try and enjoy it.

Vera: Having experienced it once, it'll be easier to tune into that feeling again. I was thinking this must be great for people who have problems staying awake at concerts. It would be perfect for them because you could just do anything. Nobody would know if you were snoozing or not.

Tim: Funny you should think about sleep because the darkness made it feel like it was much more of your own experience. Like being in your own bed, but sitting up. But the bizarreness of the situation was a bit distracting. I mean, you don't normally share such utter complete darkness with total strangers.

Vera:	But didn't you get used to the idea and let yourself be taken over by the situation?
Tim:	Yes, but then I started thinking about what it must be like for the musicians. They can probably let go a bit more because they know people aren't peering at them.
Vera:	Not only that, it must be marvellous for the performers in a different way too because surely the real essence of music is to hear what is being played. So vision is only an aid when you hear music. The hearing is the most important thing. So maybe this is a good experiment.
Tim:	Do you think the same experiment could be applied to a play? The actors could perhaps concentrate more in the darkness; lose themselves in the part. But I think it would very much depend on which play it was and to a great extent, vision is an integral part of plays, isn't it?
Vera:	Yes, there was a performance of certain speeches from Shakespeare in the dark earlier this year. It was part of this series of events entitled 'Entertainment in the Dark'. But I wonder what would happen if the actor dried up? No one would know where they were. It's not the same either, going to a play and listening to music. I'm not convinced it would be a winner.
Tim:	But wherever you are, it's true that when one of your senses is shut down, as it were, you're given the opportunity to explore the use of your other senses. Hearing as a sense is quite subdued. In our world of screens and visual images I think, these days, vision is probably the dominant sense.
Vera:	But I do like this idea of playing with the senses of sight and sound. The next event in this series is going to be 'Dinners in the Dark'. Guests eat a whole meal which is served to them in the dark.
Tim:	That's interesting because presumably people will go less for the food than for the fun of the event and you'd be more physically involved. I mean, you'd have to put something in your mouth without even knowing what it was going to be. A bit too gimmicky, perhaps?
Vera:	I'm sure you'd taste food like never before if this experience is anything to go by.
Tim:	Shall we go to that then?
Vera:	I'd love to.

[pause]

Now you'll hear Part Four again.

tone

[The recording is repeated.]

[pause]

That's the end of Part Four.

There will now be a pause of five minutes for you to copy your answers onto the separate answer sheet. Be sure to follow the numbering of all the questions.

Note: Teacher, stop the recording here and time five minutes. Remind students when there is **one** minute remaining.

[pause]

That's the end of the test. Please stop now. Your supervisor will now collect all the question papers and answer sheets.

Test 3 Key

Paper 1   Reading (1 hour 30 minutes)

Part 1   (one mark for each correct answer)

1 D	2 A	3 A	4 D	5 B	6 C	7 B	8 C	9 D
10 C	11 B	12 B	13 B	14 C	15 B	16 D	17 A	
18 D								

Part 2   (two marks for each correct answer)

19 A	20 B	21 D	22 A	23 C	24 B	25 B	26 D

Part 3   (two marks for each correct answer)

27 C	28 G	29 A	30 F	31 B	32 D	33 H

Part 4   (two marks for each correct answer)

34 B	35 C	36 D	37 A	38 B	39 A	40 C

Paper 2   Writing (2 hours)

Task-specific mark schemes

Question 1: Education

Content

Major points for discussion:
- much of what we learn in school is a waste of time
- we are motivated to learn what is relevant and useful
- what things should we learn in school

Range
Language for expressing and supporting opinions. Language for making recommendations.

Appropriacy of register and format
Register consistently appropriate for letter to newspaper.

Organisation and cohesion
Early reference to reason for writing. Well organised with an appropriate conclusion.

Target reader
Would understand the writer's point of view.

Question 2: Commemorating an achievement

Content
Proposal to suggest who should be chosen and how their life should be celebrated.

Range
Language of suggestion, explanation and recommendation.

Appropriacy of register and format
Register consistently appropriate for proposal to city council.

Organisation and cohesion
Clearly organised suggestions, possibly with headings/sub-headings.

Target reader
Would be informed.

Question 3: A Museum or Exhibition

Content
Description of contents of museum or exhibition. Evaluation of museum or exhibition. Explanation of role of museums or exhibitions in national culture.

Range
Language of description, evaluation and explanation.

Appropriacy of register and format
Consistently appropriate for review in magazine.

Organisation and cohesion
Clearly organised ideas. Adequately paragraphed.

Target reader
Would be informed about museum or exhibition and understand writer's point of view.

Question 4: Leisure activities

Content
Description of writer's favourite leisure pursuit.

Range
Language of description and possibly narration. Language of recommendation.

Appropriacy of register and format
Register consistently appropriate for magazine.

Organisation and cohesion
Clear organisation. Adequate use of paragraphing.

Target reader
Would be encouraged to take up activity described.

Question 5(a): The Accidental Tourist

Content
- description of Alexander's birth and problems as a baby which have made Muriel uncharacteristically careful and concerned about him
- the concerns she displays for his health and his appearance
- the results of this upbringing, perceived by Macon – Alexander's lack of interest, energy, enthusiasm; these are clearly shown in the effect Macon is able to have
- Alexander has new clothes, new interest (in tools, etc.) and is less bullied

Range
Language of description, narration and analysis.

Appropriacy of register and format
Consistent register, suitable for essay.

Organisation and cohesion
Suitable introduction and conclusion, well paragraphed.

Target reader
Would understand writer's view of Alexander's upbringing.

Question 5(b): The Go-Between

Content
- narration of events which reveal attitudes and conventions
- description of relationships between characters

Range
Language of narration, description and suggestion/persuasion.

Appropriacy of register and format
Appropriate to fellow members of reading group. Possibly informal, but should be consistent.

Organisation and cohesion
Well organised with suitable paragraphing or section breaks for the report.

Target reader
Would be in a position to decide whether the novel was suitable.

Question 5(c): The Colour of Blood

Content
Description of Cardinal Bem's character showing how he displays qualities that make him a hero.

Range
Language of discussion, narration and evaluation.

Appropriacy of register and format
Consistently appropriate to an arts magazine.

Organisation and cohesion
Clearly organised and paragraphed. Clear presentation of ideas.

Target reader
Would understand the writer's evaluation of the character.

Paper 3   Use of English (1 hour 30 minutes)

Part 1   (one mark for each correct answer)

1 another   **2** every   **3** whether   **4** saying   **5** at
6 came / comes   **7** anything   **8** only   **9** between   **10** apart
11 but   **12** nor / neither   **13** not   **14** were   **15** unable

Part 2   (one mark for each correct answer)

16 unrelated   **17** historians   **18** philosophical   **19** undertaken
20 revolutionary   **21** replacement   **22** innovator(s)   **23** fruitful
24 strengthened   **25** reliance

Part 3   (two marks for each correct answer)

26 count   **27** lines   **28** state   **29** impression   **30** question
31 tore

Part 4   (one mark for each correct section)

32 (almost / virtually) no OR hardly / scarcely any OR (very / precious) little OR
n't / not any call (1) + for (1)
33 it clear (that) you have (1) + the / every / a right to (1) OR it clear (that) it is (1)
+ your right to (1) OR clear (1) + your right to (1)
34 Martina's great annoyance (1) + her son had (1)
35 no circumstances (1) + is this / the door (ever) to be (1)
36 is bound (1) + to have finished the / his / her report (1)
37 a matter of time (1) + until / before she becomes / is (1)
38 are / will be subject (1) + to delay(s) (1)
39 is of no / little consequence (1) + to me which / what (1)

Part 5   (questions 40–43 two marks for each correct answer)

40 he only found bad programmes / he couldn't find any good examples (of the
various types of television programmes)
41 there is a two-way relationship between people and TV, e.g. how we are
affected by TV and how TV is affected by us
42 (he is sometimes in a position to show us that) they do not have very good
taste
43 (on) intimate terms (with the celebrity)
privy to (all kinds of personal details)
44 The paragraph should include the following points:
  i   it can shape / reshape / inform public opinion (helps people to understand
      and consider social and political issues)
  ii it can reflect / be a measure of public opinion (by measuring preferences to
      shows, public opinion can be revealed)
  iii it encourages viewers to identify with programmes / characters / celebrities
      (enables the public to know and understand celebrities)
  iv it makes certain people famous (creates celebrities)
  v   it takes the place of real-life social relations / surrogate acquaintances
      (promotes a substitute for social interaction)

Paper 4 Listening (40 minutes approximately)

Part 1   (one mark for each correct answer)
1 B   2 C   3 C   4 A   5 A   6 B   7 B   8 C

Part 2   (one mark for each correct answer)
9 rubber   10 markets   11 contamination / pollution   12 legal
13 public relations   14 (sick) sheep   15 clean environment
16 determination   17 charming

Part 3   (one mark for each correct answer)
18 B   19 C   20 B   21 A   22 C

Part 4   (one mark for each correct answer)
23 A   24 B   25 C   26 B   27 B   28 A

Transcript   *Certificate of Proficiency in English Listening Test. Test 3.*

I'm going to give you the instructions for this test.

I'll introduce each part of the test and give you time to look at the questions.

At the start of each piece you'll hear this sound:

tone

You'll hear each piece twice.

Remember, while you're listening, write your answers on the question paper.

You'll have five minutes at the end of the test to copy your answers onto the separate answer sheet.

There will now be a pause. Please ask any questions now, because you must not speak during the test.

[pause]

PART 1   *Now open your question paper and look at Part One.*

[pause]

You'll hear four different extracts. For questions 1 to 8, choose the answer (A, B or C) which fits best according to what you hear. There are two questions for each extract.

Extract 1   [pause]

tone

Let's not forget that there are lots of dedicated actors… actors who would never dream of abandoning their chosen profession, who are living with a vast ambition tucked securely under their skin, an undying hope that their turn will come one day… but at the same time, they have a restlessness about them, a desire to know more about the wider world… to go through things that they can then bring back into the theatre. It's that kind of motivation that accounts for the numbers of actors you find in offices and other workplaces, more than having a family to keep, or expensive outgoings.

The actors in the happiest position are those who – maybe through their own endeavours, maybe through their agents' – manage to find a specialism in sidelines, I mean connected with acting… radio commercials, voice-overs for TV, commentaries for films, teaching at drama schools… and so on… it might be being the presenter of audio-visuals for internal commercial use… whatever. Mostly, these jobs require expert use of the voice and mostly they're well paid.

[pause]

tone

[The recording is repeated.]

[pause]

Extract 2   [pause]

tone

Interviewer: As far as I'm concerned, all muzak should be banned. I cannot stand having to listen to that awful bland sound wherever I am. Now Richard Atwell has come up with a new form of muzak. So, Richard, why is your muzak any different?
Richard: Well, I call it 'new art muzak'. The idea is to match the exact environment with the right kind of muzak. The problem with muzak as it stands is it's a bit too general, it's just this wash of sound, usually to cover up the embarrassing lack of sound and – um – the audiences just usually get very tired of it.
Interviewer: But why do we want to cover up the lack of sound? What's wrong with silence?
Richard: Silence is good – in certain areas. In restaurants for example, I don't want to hear muzak because I'm concentrating on my other senses, taste and smell, and on the conversation. But you could use it in the retail environment.
Interviewer: Ah, but that's when it's at its worst. It's either thoroughly irritating or it's manipulative and either one is unacceptable.
Richard: No – it's designed to improve your environment.
Interviewer: Hmm…

[pause]

tone

[The recording is repeated.]

[pause]

Extract 3   [pause]

tone

Today we're going to look at the issue of concentration. Let's start with some basic exercises. OK, so, now, try to think of anything you would like to think about for five consecutive minutes, uninterrupted. First perhaps something that happened last week, then try something from a few months ago... move up to thinking through an argument, or going through all the details of a particular activity. Work in stages, starting with doing this at home, with your eyes closed... make it more difficult by trying it in a bus or a train, somewhere crowded, and then for longer at a time.

We can all concentrate when the mood takes us. For example, when you've been to a film that's really moving, one that really gets to you, and you come out into the street afterwards, your mind is very focused. For you, the people you pass in the street, the lighted shop windows... taxis swishing by... it's all still in the film, still has a heightened dramatic significance – and you are part of that drama.

[pause]

tone

[The recording is repeated.]

[pause]

Extract 4   [pause]

tone

Interviewer:	And now, a man very much in the news, Toby Hobson, joins me. Toby – 'theatre is boring' you're quoted as saying in today's newspaper. Why did you say it?
Toby:	What I actually said, Pam, was that eight out of ten productions I see I find rather tedious.
Interviewer:	Well, tedious or boring, we're splitting hairs here. I mean, you're a theatre man, you've got on well in the theatre, so why are you getting at your own side?
Toby:	Well, let me say one thing. I'm not putting myself above this premise. I've had 36 plays performed in...
Interviewer:	... Sure, but what tends to go wrong in your view?
Toby:	Well, it's a multitude of things. Either plays are inaccessible or the balance is not right between the comedy and the humanity, or the director's interpretation is too evident, or the writer's voice comes through where the character's voice should be heard. And in London seats cost a fortune, so expectations are high.

[pause]

tone

[The recording is repeated.]

That's the end of Part One.

Now turn to Part Two.

[pause]

PART 2

You will hear part of a radio programme about a wildlife conservation project located in a disused industrial port. For questions 9 to 17, complete the sentences with a word or short phrase.

You now have forty-five seconds in which to look at Part Two.

[pause]

tone

Interviewer:	In today's programme, we're visiting the once-flourishing port of Harford, now home to the Marine Wildlife Trust, and I have with me Tony Trotter, the Trust's local manager. Tony, this was once quite a sizeable port complex, wasn't it?
Tony:	Yes. Harford used to be one of the biggest oil-refining centres in the country, but since the decline of the oil industry, and the even older rubber processing in this area, it's become something of a backwater.
Interviewer:	Now, we're looking into a large tank.
Tony:	Yes, it's part of the disused oil terminal in the dockland complex – and it's where five grey seals are living at the moment.
Interviewer:	Tony, what are you doing with five seals in an oil terminal?
Tony:	Well, when the port was decommissioned some eight years ago – mostly due to shrinking markets, although there were also problems with the depth of the water in the harbour, the port owners were left with several unwanted buildings. At about the same time, the Marine Wildlife Trust was formed by a group of people who wanted to increase understanding of sea-water contamination. One of the group's first projects was finding somewhere to house five seals that needed medical care, and they approached the port owners for ideas.
Interviewer:	And they were willing to help?
Tony:	Well, not at first – after all it wasn't the kind of use they'd had in mind for their disused installations; and they had concerns about... about things like the legal considerations. But they were brought round eventually.
Interviewer:	What convinced them, do you think?
Tony:	Well, Trust members were able to point to a couple of other similar high-profile projects in other parts of the world and I think they began to see the potential public relations benefits.
Interviewer:	Tell us about the five seals here.
Tony:	Well, the handsome youngster you see here is Rory and he's about four years old. He's very typical of the animals we get here; he came to us a couple of weeks ago suffering from a viral infection which had been giving him a lot of trouble. It comes from sheep.
Interviewer:	Really?
Tony:	Yes, and it's very common amongst seals because sick sheep are especially prone to falling off cliffs into the sea. Along with poisoning from chemical waste, these viruses are the main ailments we see.
Interviewer:	How do you treat them?
Tony:	Antibiotics don't work for these conditions, but they're seldom terminal, as long as they get good food, plus a clean environment, most of the seals come through well and can be released back into the sea.
Interviewer:	Do you like this job?

Tony: Yes. I trained as a vet and I feel I have the right background. But apart from that, I obviously need a good understanding of toxins, and of course it takes plenty of determination as well. The seals that come here tend to be highly strung and not averse to giving you a strong nip, not necessarily out of malice, but, you know, they've suffered and are therefore, a bit unpredictable. So they're not quite as charming as people might think at first, they're very strong-minded.

Interviewer: Well, Tony thanks very much for showing me round. I hope they're all on the mend soon.

Tony: Thank you.

[pause]

Now you'll hear Part Two again.

tone

[The recording is repeated.]

[pause]

That's the end of Part Two.

Now turn to Part Three.

[pause]

PART 3   *You will hear part of an interview in which a professor of sociology is talking about the subject of leisure in Britain. For questions 18 to 22, choose the answer (A, B, C or D) which fits best according to what you hear.*

You now have one minute in which to look at Part Three.

[pause]

tone

Interviewer: This week we're taking a look at leisure. Joining me to decide how people behave themselves at play, and why, is Professor of Sociology at the University of Wessex, Richard Marshall. Let me start by asking you, Richard, why we need leisure in our lives at all.

Richard: Well, one interesting thing about leisure is that the word 'leisure' doesn't appear in every other language. Dutch for instance doesn't have it, but it has the term 'free time', while our word 'leisure' comes from Middle French meaning 'licence', something permitted. So the notion of freedom is at the heart of leisure. The problem is that, depending on our personal circumstances, we're only free to join in certain kinds of activities. But more and more, leisure is being seen as something where people can take control and find their own identity. Perhaps sometimes it's a response for those who are fed up at work or don't have high enough status to break through some of the boundaries; boundaries of status and the workplace, even the family...

Interviewer: I was going to say, does it relate to the way we behave at work? Do we deliberately choose something far more aspirational than our daily work?

Richard: Well, there are cases of that. There are some people who get involved in what some American sociologists have called 'serious leisure', where, for them, leisure turns into the all-consuming purpose. So work is just a place to get out of quickly with your pay packet in order to really enjoy yourself, for instance, in the amateur dramatic society or the choir.

Interviewer: But isn't it curious that we may have a very rule-filled life at work, but yet we choose a leisure activity that is also full of rules and constrictions?

Richard: Well, it's one of the great paradoxes of leisure that that idea of freedom is at the heart of it, but the further people get into particular types of leisure, the more they seem to want... um... security, and strangely, you know, whether it's shopping or going to the sports game, there are regular sorts of repeated rituals that in a way underlie these leisure activities. And you see, it's no different to many other spheres of life where, in lots of respects, you balance the excitement of the unknown and the potentially dangerous against the security of the known and the... er... normal.

Interviewer: And yet in Britain, we're still quite formal about what we call 'leisure', aren't we? Watching television, for example, is our major leisure activity, isn't it, and one which spans all ages and classes, I would guess. But we're strangely reluctant to admit that that's what we really spend a large proportion of our free time doing.

Richard: Well, a lot of people do admit it – polls show us that – but they want to say that they're doing something else. Or they admit it but they feel guilty about being a couch potato. But of course there's more than just that passive act itself in television watching. People take it into all sorts of other spheres like the workplace, or... um... other leisure activities – it's what people talk about. What would they talk about if they didn't have those sort of things to exchange?

Interviewer: And in a way the leisure place is somewhere where we transcend ourselves, we become the person we couldn't be at work.

Richard: Well, that's true, especially in some of the more dramatic examples of serious leisure. 'Uniform' leisure provides some quite interesting cases. There are different examples of activities where uniforms and dressing up, the sense of collectivity with others, apart from the status-defining uniform of the workplace are very important in terms of the respect people have for themselves.

Interviewer: But people don't always take up the leisure activities on offer, do they?

[pause]

Now you'll hear Part Three again.

tone

[The recording is repeated.]

[pause]

That's the end of Part Three.

Now turn to Part Four.

[pause]

PART 4   *You will hear part of a radio programme in which two writers discuss the appeal of the short story. For questions 23 to 28, decide whether the opinions are expressed by only one of the speakers, or whether the speakers agree. Write C for Claire, A for Alan, or B for both, where they agree.*

You now have thirty seconds in which to look at Part Four.

[pause]

tone

Presenter: Now the short story is always a popular form and never more so than at the moment. Earlier today Claire Rose, poet turned short story writer, and Alan Wood, whose third collection of short stories is just coming out, came into the studio to discuss the perennial appeal of the short story. Claire began by telling us why she writes short stories rather than novels.

Claire: First of all, it happened by accident really, I was writing poetry and it seemed natural to try and write short stories and then I continued with the short story. What about you Alan?

Alan: Well, I relish it in the same way I appreciate small portions of fine food rather than a lot of the same thing and I feel the need to stay with the short story while it still interests me.

Claire: Well, as for my latest short story, the content really lent itself to the form. There was a limited amount of information I could get about this nineteenth-century person and once I had all the information in front of me, I thought this could be incorporated in a limited space and that seemed to be the way to do it.

Alan: That was a brilliant story! Now reviews of both our work tend to describe, rather misleadingly, what we write as monologues, because, I suppose, they don't seem to have much plot in the old-fashioned sense, do they?

Claire: Not in the old-fashioned sense but I wouldn't particularly call them monologues, they're first person narratives. The fact that I've used a first person speaking voice is just because that seemed to be the best way to tell a particular story.

Alan: Mmm… it was the most intelligent response to the subject in fact.

Claire: And shifting between different narrators is the fascination for me and I think that's probably why I've stayed with the short story because it's allowed me to step into the shoes of somebody else for a little bit and there again, step out at the other end.

Alan: As you're a poet, as well, do you find the two forms overlap at all?

Claire: Well, I think there is definitely a similarity and perhaps more of a similarity between poetry and short stories than between short stories and novels.

Alan: There's an intensity in both, isn't there? Now, traditionally people often start out writing short stories before they write full-length novels. Do you think the short story is a good form for beginners?

Claire: Well, in a practical sense, in that it takes less time to write a short story than a novel, but it's not necessarily easier and I don't think it necessarily teaches you things you need to know about a novel, how to intertwine plots without losing the thread.

Alan: Writing a novel involves keeping something going, it involves opening out a narrative rather than closing in, which is what I think the short story does best.

Claire: Fortunately for us, short stories are in at the moment, aren't they? Do you think it reflects a desire to get away from the blockbuster?

Alan: Perhaps it's easier to find time to read short stories in a stressed life, perhaps people's attention spans are getting shorter, or perhaps it's because now you can pick up a paperback in the supermarket with your weekly shop.

Claire: It's more that some shops will put the short stories by the till and you know people buy them with that last three pounds or whatever. It's the spend factor.

Alan: But… um, you know, I like writing them, so perhaps it's just because people like reading them. There must be something in the form itself rather than it's just a nice little story.

Claire: Well, whatever it is, it's clearly a genre that is flourishing…

[pause]

Now you'll hear Part Four again.

tone

[The recording is repeated.]

[pause]

That's the end of Part Four.

There will now be a pause of five minutes for you to copy your answers onto the separate answer sheet. Be sure to follow the numbering of all the questions.

Note: Teacher, stop the recording here and time five minutes. Remind students when there is **one** minute remaining.

[pause]

That's the end of the test. Please stop now. Your supervisor will now collect all the question papers and answer sheets.

Test 4 Key

Paper 1 Reading (1 hour 30 minutes)

Part 1 (one mark for each correct answer)

1 C   2 D   3 A   4 C   5 B   6 B   7 C   8 D   9 D
10 B   11 A   12 C   13 B   14 C   15 A   16 D   17 A
18 B

Part 2 (two marks for each correct answer)

19 D   20 B   21 A   22 B   23 A   24 C   25 D   26 B

Part 3 (two marks for each correct answer)

27 E   28 H   29 B   30 G   31 A   32 F   33 C

Part 4 (two marks for each correct answer)

34 A   35 B   36 C   37 C   38 B   39 D   40 A

Paper 2 Writing (2 hours)

Task-specific mark schemes

Question 1: Consumer choice

Content
Writer's own opinions on the following three influences of consumer choice.

Major points for discussion:
- own desires
- media
- friends

Range
Language for expressing and supporting opinions.

Appropriacy of register and format
Format appropriate to an article (may have headings/sub-headings). Register consistent and appropriate for a general interest magazine.

Organisation and cohesion
Adequately paragraphed. Suitable conclusion.

Target reader
Would be interested and would understand the writer's views.

Question 2: A day that changed my life for the better

Content
Description of the day. Explanation of how life changed for the better. Reason(s) why life changed (experience must be believable).

Range
Language of narration, description, explanation and evaluation.

Appropriacy of register and format
Letter opening and closing conventions not essential. Register appropriate to letter to a magazine. Register consistent throughout.

Organisation and cohesion
Appropriate introduction – reason for writing. Clearly organised in paragraphs. Balance between description/explanation. Appropriate conclusion.

Target reader
Would understand the events of the day and their effect on the writer and would appreciate the writer's positive reaction.

Question 3: Television viewing habits

Content
Aspects of television in writer's country – variety of programmes – popularity of various programme types – role of television in people's lives.

Range
Language of description, giving information, analysing, evaluating – vocabulary connected with types of television programmes, e.g. documentaries, news bulletins, etc.

Appropriacy of register and format
Report format – may include headings/sub-headings. Appropriate register – formal and objective. Register consistent throughout.

Organisation and cohesion
Suitable introduction – giving purpose of report. Clearly organised in sections.

Target reader
Would be well informed about the nature of television programmes in the writer's country and the role of television in people's lives.

Question 4: Festivals and customs from around the world

Content
Proposal should include information about festivals and customs and how these maintain traditions.

Range
Language for making and supporting suggestions.

Appropriacy of register and format
Proposal format, possibly with headings/sub-headings. Formal register. Register consistent throughout.

Organisation and cohesion
Suitable introduction and conclusion.

Target reader
Would understand the customs and festivals described. Would understand how these maintain traditions in writer's country. Would understand why the writer feels these should be included in the book.

Question 5(a): The Colour of Blood

Content
Essay must explain why the two, General Francis Urban and Jop, help Bem and describe the form their help takes.
Brief description of the situation:
- all three are determined to avoid conflict and bloodshed
How Urban helps, e.g.:
- gives Bem 24 hours, money and a safe telephone number
- provides guards to keep Bem safe so that he can preach 'no revolution'
- himself attends the Rywald service
How Jop helps, e.g.:
- promises to tell the union leaders that the strike is not Bem's idea and does not have his support
- arranges transport to Gneisk
(Underlined points must be included – bulleted points are suggested relevant information.)

Range
Language of narration, description and explanation.

Appropriacy of register and format
Register suitable for essay for tutor. Register consistent throughout.

Organisation and cohesion
Well organised in paragraphs.

Target reader
Would understand why Urban and Jop help Bem and how they do this.

Question 5(b): The Accidental Tourist

Content
Review must describe the Leary family background and Macon's escape from it:
Family background:
- Macon's mother and father
- the grandparents
- the children – self-sufficient, inward-looking (e.g. card game, not answering the telephone, etc.)
Influence on Macon, e.g.:
- domestic arrangements when Sarah leaves
- concept of the tourist guides
- desire to organise and control
- remaining untouched by outward events

Escape, e.g.:
- fortuitous meeting with Muriel
- dog training – Muriel's ideas (what Martians would think of Earth)
- Muriel's calming influence during panic attack
- her influence grows until he can tell her about Ethan
- change in Macon (eats pizza with his fingers, etc.)
- Macon begins to feel manipulated
- in Paris realises that he has never initiated anything in his life
- finally acts decisively

(Underlined points must be included – bulleted points are suggested relevant information.)

Range
Language of description, narration and explanation.

Appropriacy of register and format
Register and format consistent and appropriate for a review for a tutor.

Organisation and cohesion
Suitable introduction. Clearly organised and presented as a review.

Target reader
Would have a clear picture of the Leary family, understand its influence on Macon and realise how he escapes.

Question 5(c): The Go-Between

Content
The article must describe Leo's visit, explain its effect on him and show how it was a turning point in his life:
- the setting – early twentieth century, country house, parties, etc.

Leo's life before visit, e.g.:
- with his mother in Salisbury
- prep. school with rules, rituals and conventions

The visit, e.g.:
- more rules and rituals
- boys left to their own devices
- visit to Norwich
- Leo as postman
- cricket match
- picnics

Effect on Leo:
- he is used by Ted and Marian
- deception – only Ted explains things to him
- Marian is purely selfish
- he is confused by the unfamiliar conventions
- final scene – destroys his belief in beauty, godlike figures of the Zodiac

Consequences:
- Leo's life becomes one devoted to facts
- he never marries, has no relationships

(Underlined points must be included – bulleted points are suggested relevant information.)

Range
Language of description, narration and explanation.

Appropriacy of register and format
Format suited to magazine article. Register suited to magazine readers. Register consistent throughout.

Organisation and cohesion
Clearly paragraphed. Balance between narration and explanation.

Target reader
Would understand what happened during visit, the effect it had on Leo and how it changed his life.

Paper 3 Use of English (1 hour 30 minutes)

Part 1 (one mark for each correct answer)

1 where 2 come 3 without 4 part 5 when / if 6 to
7 as 8 get 9 at 10 before 11 whom 12 long 13 his
14 resulted / ended / culminated / climaxed 15 this

Part 2 (one mark for each correct answer)

16 package 17 erosion 18 moisture 19 droughts
20 existence 21 exceptionally 22 substantial 23 sensitive
24 research 25 gathering

Part 3 (two marks for each correct answer)

26 open 27 gathered 28 support 29 order 30 mystery
31 stand

Part 4 (one mark for each correct section)

32 has declined (1) + during / over / in the past / last (1)
33 to drop us (1) + a line (in order) (1)
34 Jane's failure (1) + to reply to his invitation / invite (1)
35 the old vase could / might (possibly) be (1) + made into (1)
36 in the habit (1) + of playing (1)
37 the height of (1) + his success (1)
38 the (vast) majority of (the) students (1) + Shula makes (1)
39 impressed by / at / with (1) OR impressed to see (1) + (just) how skilled / skilful / skilful a (1)

Part 5 (questions 40–43 two marks for each correct answer)

40 the work needed in order to (be able to) make predictions
41 (he wishes to emphasise that) scientists are not just making excuses AND/OR scientists really do need to do more work / research
42 (but only that their) discipline is very young

43 the work that scientists do (e.g. making advances, finding explanations, working out rules) is complex AND/OR based on limited information / evidence / data
44 The paragraph should include the following points:
   i   scientific explanations are rarely final – each explanation raises new questions
   ii some branches of science are fairly new / young (e.g. ecology / geoscience) Scientists find new areas / branches to study
   iii there's a lot we don't know about the world / the world which scientists are trying to explain is extremely complex
   iv (whenever / frequently / all the time) things (evidence / events) occur which cannot be explained by existing (scientific) theory and this leads to more activity / knowledge
   v   thousands of people are involved in scientific work / new (collaborative) ways of working produce more (complex) theories / questions / problems (for scientists to resolve)

Paper 4   Listening (40 minutes approximately)

Part 1   (one mark for each correct answer)
1 A   2 B   3 B   4 C   5 C   6 A   7 C   8 A

Part 2   (one mark for each correct answer)
9 bakery / baker's   10 blankets   11 (their / the) body heat
12 (the) skin   13 (some) shelter / shelters   14 (the) grass
15 guest house   16 intelligence   17 humming / hum

Part 3   (one mark for each correct answer)
18 B   19 A   20 A   21 C   22 D

Part 4   (one mark for each correct answer)
23 G   24 B   25 M   26 B   27 B   28 G

Transcript   *Certificate of Proficiency in English Listening Test. Test 4.*

I'm going to give you the instructions for this test.

I'll introduce each part of the test and give you time to look at the questions.

At the start of each piece you'll hear this sound:

tone

You'll hear each piece twice.

Remember, while you're listening, write your answers on the question paper.

You'll have five minutes at the end of the test to copy your answers onto the separate answer sheet.

There will now be a pause. Please ask any questions now, because you must not speak during the test.

[pause]

PART 1   *Now open your question paper and look at Part One.*

[pause]

You'll hear four different extracts. For questions 1 to 8, choose the answer (A, B or C) which fits best according to what you hear. There are two questions for each extract.

Extract 1   [pause]

tone

When the artist Andy Warhol predicted that everyone would get their fifteen minutes of fame, even he can't have seen that now some would expect their full hour – and a spread in a magazine. Fame has certainly changed over the years. If you look at what passes for stars these days, we seem to have lost two things. One is a sense of mystery, there's a voracious appetite to know more about people now – in the golden age of Hollywood in the 1930s and 40s, stars were at a distance, they were magical. And we've also lost the ability to distinguish between fame and notoriety. Now, if you catch the public eye, you're famous, you're a celebrity – no matter what you've done.

    And then what happens is that after their fifteen minutes of fame, unless the celebrity has had the sense to capitalise on it, and do something worthwhile, for example open a restaurant or write a book, they fade away, because there is too much competition out there and there is always another up-and-coming star to replace them.

[pause]

tone

[The recording is repeated.]

[pause]

Extract 2   [pause]

tone

Interviewer: Drumkits improved quite rapidly in the 1920s, but many of the innovations in drumkits were very much homemade and done on the road. Hard to trace who thought up the new inventions, although musicians say a lot of the credit should go to a studio drummer called Vic Burton. Here's his brother Ralph:

Ralph: If you look at pictures of dance orchestras before about 1920, you'll see the drummer has two cymbals, those thin round plates of brass that give out that satisfying 'crash!' or 'zing!' when he hits them. The big crash cymbal hangs from a contraption atop the bass drum, the other smaller 'zinger' is screwed to the rim of the bass drum. So far as I know, nobody before Vic realised there was no place in the modern dance sound for that thin tinkle. The little 'zinger' had to go! So he removed it from the old spot and put it on top of the bass drum alongside the big crash cymbal, where it could be played as an independent instrument. Soon every drummer in the business had his cymbals positioned like this. Vic went on to…

[pause]

tone

[The recording is repeated.]

[pause]

Extract 3
[pause]

tone

Interviewer: Well, personally, Ian, I thought some of the visual effects in the film were rather overdone, particularly when the camera goes inside the main character's head, to show us that, you know, he sees his own world in terms of a computer game.

Ian: Contrived, wasn't it? Or perhaps the director was trying to play too much to the target youth audience. Otherwise the use of computer-generated images and lighting seemed inventive and exuberant. There it felt desperate, as if they were thinking, 'How do we jazz up this moment?'

But the underlying problem is that Mark, the 'hero', shouldn't have been isolated from the rest of his community for so long that he becomes psychotic in a way that seems to exonerate him from all blame. And the fact that he snaps back into being a morally responsible being after having committed an act of violence seemed a cop-out and superfluous, because there's plenty of tension already. We don't need his interior darkness, there's enough communal darkness. And I think the idea of the whole community being compromised by their actions without any individual cracking up is actually more powerful.

[pause]

tone

[The recording is repeated.]

[pause]

Extract 4
[pause]

tone

The professionals – Wyndham United – again progressed against the plucky opposition of amateur team Longbridge. This time Wyndham United's Martin Butler's goal was the decisive touch. In the first half, Wyndham United lived a tad dangerously with Longbridge's chance coming in a bright opening ten minutes after the start of the game, with Whitaker's kick just missing the open goal. Wyndham United struggled to half-time and beyond without too much to thrill but, slowly but surely, as the amateurs tired, the Wyndham stamina began to pay dividends as they pushed them further and further back. Some of the players fought a spiteful battle all afternoon, sadly ignored by the referee. In particular Baldwin, whose foul on the star player Smithson in the forty-first minute was finally enough to warrant the referee's intervention. Not a pretty match, but it'll do.

[pause]

tone

[The recording is repeated.]

That's the end of Part One.

Now turn to Part Two.

[pause]

PART 2
You will hear an interview with Peter Simon, a farmer from Scotland who keeps llamas – animals which are native to South America. For questions 9 to 17, complete the sentences with a word or short phrase.

You now have forty-five seconds in which to look at Part Two.

[pause]

tone

Interviewer:	Today I'm visiting Peter and Ann Simon who own a small farm in Scotland. However, it is no run-of-the-mill farm as their livestock is a type of animal which is usually associated with South America, the llama. Peter, you're originally from London so how did you end up here in Scotland with these engaging creatures?
Peter:	Living in London was becoming increasingly stressful because of transport, finances, etc., so we opted out of the family bakery business, where I did the accounts and my wife the marketing. We were fed up of the whole rat race thing and just headed for the hills.
Interviewer:	And what made you choose to spend your days with llamas?
Peter:	Well, Ann has started a little cottage industry, weaving, and she needed some robust fleece for the blankets she makes and llamas seemed to be an interesting alternative to sheep. So we got them about three years ago.
Interviewer:	And do they fit in pretty well up here?
Peter:	Oh yes, being creatures accustomed to high altitude they happily sit through the Scottish wind and blizzards. During winter snowstorms they can be found serenely sitting out the blizzard. The long hollow structure of the fibre of their fleeces makes sure that they retain body heat.
Interviewer:	So you haven't had any problems with them?
Peter:	Well, in fact we have. They seem to have trouble in constant rain because, unlike our British sheep, they don't have any natural lanolin, so they easily get saturated by repeated downpours and they started to suffer from skin diseases and they were obviously getting distressed by this.
Interviewer:	It must have been awful to see them suffer.
Peter:	Absolutely, so we had to find a cheap solution, but that was easy enough. I knocked up some shelters for them near the old barns in the bottom field.
Interviewer:	The land around here isn't known for its lush vegetation. How do they manage to feed?
Peter:	Fortunately, llamas thrive on poor vegetation; they can survive on a diet of thistles, rushes and weeds that other animals might find unpalatable. And something we hadn't bargained for is that grass is beginning to grow because grazing the llamas here is enriching the land.
Interviewer:	Are you able to make a living from Ann's weaving alone?
Peter:	We just couldn't manage and we had to find ways of boosting our finances. Funnily enough, reading about llamas in South America gave us the answer. We hit upon the idea of llama trekking so now we put people up in a converted barn which we run as a kind of guest house, and offer them trips up into the hills.
Interviewer:	And how on earth did you get the llamas to cooperate? I thought they were notoriously bad-tempered?
Peter:	They have their moments… but the thing that surprised us was their intelligence compared with… our… let's be frank… pretty stupid sheep. They proved to be ready pupils and very little initial training was needed to persuade them to carry a pack.
Interviewer:	Was it just like breaking in a horse?
Peter:	Oh, no, quite different. We had great fun and games with their training and they did need very careful handling. The method we found the most useful for getting them to trust us was humming to them. You know, they sort of hum to each other and we had to get just the right tone and try to replicate it.
Interviewer:	And can any llama be used as a pack animal?
Peter:	Well, when you start to look into it…

[pause]

Now you'll hear Part Two again.

tone

[The recording is repeated.]

[pause]

That's the end of Part Two.

Now turn to Part Three.

[pause]

PART 3   *You will hear a radio interview with Maureen Kemp, a ballet dancer. For questions 18 to 22, choose the answer (A, B, C or D) which fits best according to what you hear.*

You now have one minute in which to look at Part Three.

[pause]

tone

Interviewer: You've been a principal dancer for many years now. How did it all begin?

Maureen: When I was three, my mum decided 'Ooh, what a nice thing it would be for my little girl to go to ballet class' but I went to the sort of dancing school that did everything, you know, the tap, the singing, the modern, because a lot of girls round there, or their mums at any rate, you know, were into that, because some of them had been on stage themselves, and the ballet was, you know, rather a second thought.

Interviewer: So when did you move on to actual ballet then?

Maureen: Well, ballet was involved from the beginning, but when I was about the age of ten my teacher suggested that I tried for a scholarship at the Royal Academy of Dancing which, you know, that would entitle me to two classes a week in London. It meant I was able to stay at my normal school studying which my parents were very concerned about, you know, that I did my exams and all that and rather than go to a specialist ballet school which would have meant boarding and being away from home, you know. Anyway, I was successful in the audition and well, I had this scholarship for five years.

Interviewer: And then when you finished you were able to start a career as a professional ballet dancer?

Maureen: People say to me, you know, 'When did you decide that you were going to be a dancer?' and I rather feel that I slipped into it, you know, purely because I was enjoying it.

Interviewer: Really? Now, one of the people you worked with in your early career was David Nottley, who is now a very well-known choreographer.

Maureen: Yes, it was wonderful being young and actually working to create new dances.

Interviewer: Yes, I'm sure.

Maureen: It was also quite unusual because he was a member of the company I was working with so I knew him very well. It was wonderful to get the experience of working on newly-created pieces without actually having to meet these high-profile choreographers, you know, 'the gods', as it were.

Interviewer: And how did you prepare for these new roles? I mean is it very different... is it a very different preparation when you're doing something that no one has ever seen before?

Maureen: Well, I think that in the studio you've got to go in with a completely open mind and actually be ready to work harder than you've ever worked before because it's no good for a choreographer to try something out on you and then say, you know, 'Oh well, it's too tiring to keep doing this over and over again'. He wants to see it danced full out with no holding back and you've got to remember what he told you to do.

Interviewer: Yes.

Maureen: But you really feel by opening night that the part is really part of you. You've got the added bonus of the audience never having seen it before so they're not going to say, 'Oh I remember so-and-so when she did it', you know, so that sort of takes the nerves off of it.

Interviewer:	Yes, quite. Have you ever wanted to choreograph yourself?
Maureen:	Well, I pride myself in thinking that I'm good at taking a lead once I'm given the initial idea, and, you know, I can work on it from there but I never have that first instinctive thought in my mind, you know, the one that sets off the creative process.
Interviewer:	It's strange because you've often been described as not just being a purely classical dancer because, well, you've got all sorts of skills and acting abilities, and all sorts, haven't you?
Maureen:	I mean, I don't see myself as a classical dancer. It's like actors and actresses say, you know, it's easier to hide behind a character. I think it's the same for dancing because when you've got no character, or very little character to play, you are relying on pure technique and I'd never describe myself as what I would call a drum roll dancer, waiting for the tricks to happen.
Interviewer:	I see.
Maureen:	It just doesn't inspire me to dance well. It's when I can use a character to justify the movement, that's when I love dancing.
Interviewer:	Maureen, thank you.

[pause]

Now you'll hear Part Three again.

tone

[The recording is repeated.]

[pause]

That's the end of Part Three.

Now turn to Part Four.

[pause]

PART 4

You will hear part of a discussion in which two friends, Gordon and Martha, are discussing current issues in education. For questions 23 to 28, decide whether the opinions are expressed by only one of the speakers, or whether the speakers agree. Write G for Gordon, M for Martha, or B for both, where they agree.

You now have thirty seconds in which to look at Part Four.

[pause]

tone

Gordon:	Martha, you know the family who live opposite me, the Guthries?
Martha:	You mean the one with the twin daughters?
Gordon:	Yeah. Well I found out something really surprising today. They're taking their children out of the state school and educating them at home.
Martha:	Sorry Gordon, you mean just the two girls on their own?
Gordon:	No, they're getting together with three other families here in Oxford. And they're setting up a small school for all the children on the top floor of one of the families' houses until they can find a more suitable building. Two of the parents will be teaching part of the time and they've found a professional teacher to help them. I think it's a really exciting step.
Martha:	I suppose it is in a way. There are so many considerations though, and – um – it's a heavy responsibility to take on, on top of normal life. If I were them, I'd be concerned about the children missing out on contact with their peers.

Gordon:	Mmm. Well, the friends I made at school were certainly the best bit. But looking at some of the bigger schools we've got now, some kids don't thrive, do they? They feel vulnerable, get picked on or get into trouble. As a parent, I can see that you'd, you know, want to give your kids a secure environment to learn in.
Martha:	There is the theory that you should face up to your problems, though, and that's how you learn and – er – become stronger – the survival of the fittest.
Gordon:	The law of the jungle idea? Just think about it, kids who are turned off by a negative experience of learning, what does that lead to? Disaffection then delinquency and finally young adults who don't fit into our society and its aims. We don't want that element on our streets, do we?
Martha:	It's certainly becoming a serious issue in some places, but let's get back to what you were saying about these 'home schools'.
Gordon:	Yes, OK. Actually, I'm not sure about – um – the practicalities. For instance, it seems unlikely that one could cover the breadth of learning that children can gain in a large secondary school.
Martha:	I've heard of small home schools that take full advantage of the local community. There's one where my sister lives. They run environmental research projects, go into companies, etc. and so, there's quite a span of – er – learning opportunities for the kids to experience. But it seems clear to me as someone not involved in education, that taking advantage of a range of options is far less problematic with small groups.
Gordon:	That goes without saying. But do we actually have to stick with our enormous, unwieldy state schools with their thousands of children? I remember seeing an article about an experiment somewhere in the States, in which huge schools were being divided into small autonomous units providing better security, smaller class sizes and a closer relationship with teachers.
Martha:	Nice idea but how were they going to pay for it?
Gordon:	That part, the article wasn't very clear about…
Martha:	Typical!
Gordon:	…but I think they were going to introduce a new 'flatter' management structure or some other useless piece of jargon and, come to think of it, we know what that means – a lot of extra hassle and work for the staff but no real benefits! In other words, change for change's sake.
Martha:	You're getting cynical in your old age! If we listened to people like you, we'd still be in the Dark Ages with no education at all! But anyway how are the Guthries getting on with their home school?
Gordon:	Well, it's a bit early to tell. They've only just…

[pause]

Now you'll hear Part Four again.

tone

[The recording is repeated.]

[pause]

That's the end of Part Four.

There will now be a pause of five minutes for you to copy your answers onto the separate answer sheet. Be sure to follow the numbering of all the questions.

Note: Teacher, stop the recording here and time five minutes. Remind students when there is **one** minute remaining.

[pause]

That's the end of the test. Please stop now. Your supervisor will now collect all the question papers and answer sheets.

Sample answer sheet: Paper 1

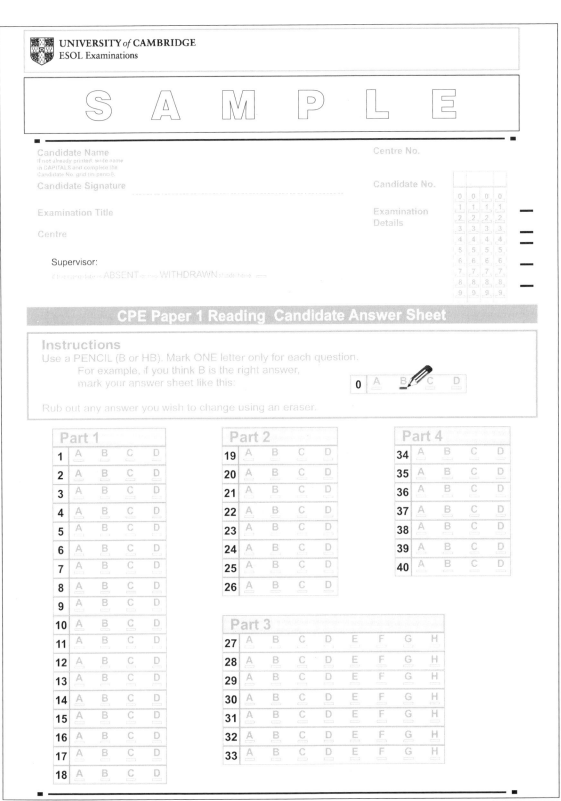

UNIVERSITY *of* **CAMBRIDGE**
ESOL Examinations

S A M P L E

Candidate Name
If not already printed, write name
in CAPITALS and complete the
Candidate No. grid (in pencil).

Candidate Signature

Examination Title

Centre

Supervisor:
If the candidate is ABSENT or has WITHDRAWN shade here

Centre No.

Candidate No.

Examination
Details

CPE Paper 3 Use of English Candidate Answer Sheet 1

Part 1

Do not write below here

Instructions

Use a PENCIL
(B or HB).

Rub out any answer
you wish to change
using an eraser.

For **Parts 1, 2** and **3**:
Write your answer
clearly in CAPITAL
LETTERS.
Write one letter in each
box.

For example:

| 0 | M A Y | | |

Answer **Parts 4 and 5**
on Answer Sheet 2.

Write your answer
neatly in the spaces
provided.

You do not have to
write in capital letters for
Parts 4 and 5.

1 2 3 4 5 6 7 8 9 10 11 12 13 14 15

157

Sample answer sheet: Paper 3

Part 2

		Do not write below here
16		1 16 0
17		1 17 0
18		1 18 0
19		1 19 0
20		1 20 0
21		1 21 0
22		1 22 0
23		1 23 0
24		1 24 0
25		1 25 0

Part 3

		Do not write below here
26		1 26 0
27		1 27 0
28		1 28 0
29		1 29 0
30		1 30 0
31		1 31 0

Continue with Parts 4 and 5 on Answer Sheet 2 ▶

UNIVERSITY *of* **CAMBRIDGE**
ESOL Examinations

S A M P L E

Candidate Name
If not already printed, write name
in CAPITALS and complete the
Candidate No. grid (in pencil)

Candidate Signature

Examination Title

Centre

Supervisor:
If the candidate is ABSENT or has WITHDRAWN shade here ◁

Centre No.

Candidate No.

Examination
Details

0	0	0	0
1	1	1	1
2	2	2	2
3	3	3	3
4	4	4	4
5	5	5	5
6	6	6	6
7	7	7	7
8	8	8	8
9	9	9	9

CPE Paper 3 Use of English Candidate Answer Sheet 2

Part 4

Do not write
below here

32		32 2 1 0
33		33 2 1 0
34		34 2 1 0
35		35 2 1 0
36		36 2 1 0
37		37 2 1 0
38		38 2 1 0
39		39 2 1 0

Sample answer sheet: Paper 3

Part 5

		Do not write below here
40		40 1 0
41		41 1 0
42		42 1 0
43		43 1 0

Part 5: question 44

For Examiner use only

Marks

Examiner number:
Team and Position

Content	0	1	2	3	4					

Language	0	1.1	1.2	2.1	2.2	3.1	3.2	4.1	4.2	5.1	5.2

0	0	0	0
1	1	1	1
2	2	2	2
3	3	3	3
4	4	4	4
5	5	5	5
6	6	6	6
7	7	7	7
8	8	8	8
9	9	9	9

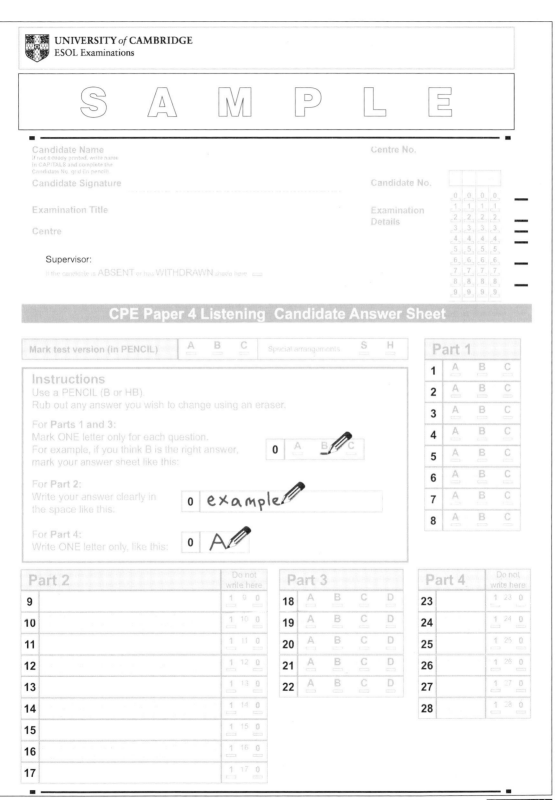